The Blood of Martyrs
... The Seed of Faith

Illustration by Kakule Mwangu Emmanuel, osc, to commemorate the 800th Jubilee of the Order of the Holy Cross in 2010.

The Blood of Martyrs...The Seed of Faith: The Hostages of Makondo

A Diary from the Period of the Simba
in the Democratic Republic of the Congo
1964–1965

By Father Jan Verhoeven, osc

Translated from the Dutch into French by Pierre-I. Magnée
Translated from the French into American English
by Father Ernest N. Martello, osc

Edited and Published by
Crosier Fathers and Brothers
Province of St. Odilia
Phoenix, AZ

The Hostages of Makondo is a diary of one of the thirty-one missionaries who were assassinated after nine months of captivity at a place called Buta by the Congolese rebels called the Simba (which in Swahili means "lion"), who are sometimes called the "Mulelists" after the name of one of their founders, Mulele. This posthumous edition is completed by the notes of Brother Lambert Schoenmakers, osc, and a report by Sister M. Eveline van Valkenborgh of the Sisters of the Heart of Mary of Berlaar in Belgium, and was prepared in French by Dries Jannsen. Fathers Jan Bierens, osc, and M. Colson, osc, took care of the introduction and commentaries.

Crosier Fathers and Brothers Province of St. Odilia
Phoenix, Arizona

Printed in the United States of America

ISBN: 978-0-9886741-0-3

Originally published as *Gijzelaars onder Makondo: Dagboek uit Simda-tijd 1964–1965* © Lichtland / Diest, 1965

English Translator's Note:
I have taken the liberty to add explanatory notes where I thought it would be useful for American readers.

Contents

Foreword

Throughout the history of Christianity, our faith community has been faithful to its tradition of telling stories. Scripture scholars are in agreement that what we have today in the four Gospel accounts of the life, ministry, passion, death, and resurrection of Jesus began as stories told over and over again, first by eyewitnesses and later by others who came to faith in Christ through their testimony. The telling of stories is a truly human and divine art form, allowing us to be in communion with the events and spirits of those who took part in those events in the past. Stories of faith invite us to taste and see the goodness of the Lord in those who have gone before us, inviting us to taste and see the same goodness in our own lives.

This book is the result of the Crosier desire to keep one of our formative stories alive to inspire faith and love for God. In these pages, the reader is invited to enter the world and experience of a group of courageous men and women who found themselves living through a period of change and confusion, tension and fear, unrest and violence. Though courageous in their faith, they felt fear and concern for their safety and the safety of the people among whom they lived and served. Father Verhoeven's testament speaks of both the ordinary and extraordinary moments during the nine-month period covered by his journal. The reader is invited to enter the world of the early 1960's in Congo that lies in the heart of the African continent.

This story is formative for us Crosiers as it brings us to the foot of the Cross, not as an object of devotion and adoration but as a mystery to be lived. In the suffering of our confreres and the others involved in this story, our spirituality of the Cross coaxes us forward to perceive the signs of hope and new life in the midst of the story. We are invited to discern the profound truth that the deeper reality is God's ability to bring life out of death, to stand firm in the conviction that what appears to be complete destruction is not the whole story. The fact that almost twenty years later, the Crosiers discovered the grace to invest significantly in the life of the Church and society in

Congo again reflects this mystery of life through death.

I am deeply grateful to our confrere, Ernest Martello, osc, for dedicating the time and energy to make this story available in English. May its telling inspire faith and love for God in lives spent in loving service.

Very Reverend Thomas A. Enneking, osc
Prior Provincial
Crosier Province of Saint Odilia
August 28, 2012

Preface

A story of the Crosier Fathers and Brothers in Africa—
the twenty-three martyrs of 1965 and the rising of the Order
in the new African members named for the martyrs,
The Proprovince of the Martyrs of Bondo

"Unless a grain of wheat falls into the ground and dies, it remains just a grain of wheat; but if it dies, it produces much fruit." John 12:24

For twenty years (1986–2006), I was assigned to the Crosier mission in the Democratic Republic of the Congo (the old Zaire, and before that the "Belgian Congo") where I was a teacher of philosophy in our college seminary, at a place called Mulo in the Province of North Kivu.

One of my most treasured memories is of a trip I made during the summer of 1990 to the northern Province of Orientale. Here I traced the footsteps of the twenty-three martyrs of the Crosier Fathers and Brothers who gave their lives in the rebellion of 1964–1965. I went to Bondo where they had lived and worked and to Buta where twenty-one of them were killed. Their memory haunted me and blessed me. Though I had never known them personally, my heart was filled with emotion, and my eyes would swell with tears as I visited every place where they had lived, were under house arrest, were imprisoned, and where they were killed.

The Crosiers had come to the Congo, at that time the Belgian Congo, in 1920 and were assigned the area north of the Uele River, in northern Congo. They worked hard preaching the Good News of Jesus Christ, baptizing many, and introducing them to the sacramental and community life of the Catholic Church. Independence of the colony from Belgium was forced in 1960 by the African and world political climate. In 1964–1965, there was a rebellion in the northern and eastern parts of the country against the new Congolese government, led by a group that called themselves the "Simba" (Swahili for "lion").

In this volume, you will find my translation from French into

English of the nine-month diary of one of the martyrs, Father Jan Verhoeven, osc, titled "The Hostages of Makondo." It was originally written in Dutch and was quickly translated into French in 1965. This is its first American translation.

His diary begins with the day of the arrival of the Simba in Bondo. The missionaries were forced to assist at the execution of some of their parishioners and friends, leaders of the people who belonged to the "wrong" political party. It was devastating to their spirits.

This begins the nine-month-long house arrest, during which, almost daily, they were harassed by the Simba. Eventually seven Brothers of Saint Gabriel and three priests of the Capuchin Order were added to the group. They endured constant searches and daily requests for batteries, radios, wristwatches, motorcycles, and bikes. At times they were relatively comfortable and well-provisioned, and yet at other times, they would be in great need of medicine, food, or decent bedding. Sometimes they were permitted to stay in their rooms and bathe in the river; at other times, they were forced together in one common room at the minor seminary or crammed into one room in a house or a prison.

The mood of the fathers and brothers was a constant roller-coaster ride as they heard of the liberation of other groups, sometimes just a few miles away or a day's ride in a jeep from where they were. One day they were hopeful, and the next their hopes fell when they were passed over or had heard of the murder of colleagues or friends. A great assault to their morale was hearing in February of the murder of two of their Crosier confreres along with an Ursuline nun and lay person on November 25, 1964, at the mission post of Dakwa.

Father Verhoeven's journal ends a couple of weeks before their massacre, and so the details of the ensuing days are filled in with other accounts. The night before the massacre, the fathers and brothers—along with the white sisters, the Congolese bishop of Buta, and two indigenous sisters—were all locked in one room alongside the Rubi River at Buta. People made their last confessions. That night the Congolese Bishop Jacques Mbali of Buta and the two indigenous sisters were released, though the bishop protested that he was ready to die if necessary. The next day, in midmorning, the white sisters were moved up to the regular prison, leaving only the missionary fathers and brothers: among them twenty-one Crosier priests and brothers, seven Brothers of Saint Gabriel, and the three Capuchin priests. Colonel Augustine Makondo, who had sworn many times that he would protect them and keep them safe, gave orders by radio as he was fleeing the area that all the white missionary men were to be executed.

Accounts of the massacre vary. It took about an hour. The most reliable account says that at five o'clock in the afternoon about fifty Simba, undoubtedly high on drugs and alcohol, came to the prison house on the banks of the Rubi River. Amid great howling and singing of patriotic songs, they forced the missionaries to undress and then tied their hands behind their backs. Led out on the banks of the river in two rows, the missionaries were also singing. Then they were taken two by two, beaten with clubs, pierced in the chest or stomach with a spear, and then thrown onto logs on the bank where their heads, along with other body parts, were chopped off with large machetes. There were a few gunshots. All the body parts were thrown into the river and disappeared, eaten by crocodiles downstream. The Simba fled. Some were killed, others executed, and still others absorbed back into their various backgrounds. Here follows the diary of Jan Verhoeven, osc.

Father Ernest N. Martello, osc
Priory of the Exaltation of the Holy Cross
Onamia, Minnesota, U.S.A.
May 3, 2012
Solemnity of the Dedication of the Churches and Priories
of the Order of the Holy Cross

A note on the use of the word "martyr": In the tradition of the Catholic Church, the term martyr *has been reserved to those who sacrifice their lives specifically for their faith. Thus they are killed because they are Catholic Christians by someone who hates the Catholic Christian faith. Sometimes they were asked to deny their faith in word or action and they refused, thus incurring martyrdom.*

The use of the word seems to be extended in our day to include those who give up their lives for their neighbors. As we read in John's Gospel: "No one has greater love than this, to lay down one's life for one's friends" (15:13). An instance of this is seen in the canonization of Saint Maximilian Kolbe, who was named a martyr because he gave his life so that another man in prison might live.

The Crosier martyrs could have taken flight at the first sign of danger, but they didn't. They decided to stay for the sake of the people. Later, sometimes they talked of escape, but always set aside the idea because of the reprisals they feared would come to the sisters or the local people. It is in this second sense, then, that we call them martyrs.

In giving them this exalted title of "martyr," we do not mean to infer that they were perfect and always did the right or best thing. They were men of their age, of European background, and part of the colonial system. Undoubtedly, they made some mistakes and realized this painfully during the time of their imprisonment. One of them, Fr. Gerard Kester, osc, left behind some notes to the effect that missionary work would never be the same. Missionaries coming later would have to collaborate and work along with the native clergy and people rather than in the colonial fashion of always considering themselves as the teachers and supervisors. That said, we still stand in admiration of their achievements as missionaries and their great courage in staying and giving their lives for their people.

Crosier Lenten Prayer in Praise of the Cross

From the Crosier Memorials of the Holy Cross

God our Savior,
in your plan of salvation
your Son Jesus Christ accepted the cross
and freed us from the power of death.

We honor the cross
as the sign of our redemption.
May we reap the harvest of salvation
planted in pain by your Son Jesus Christ.
May our sins be nailed to his cross,
the power of life released,
pride conquered,
and weakness turned to strength.

May the cross be our comfort in trouble,
our refuge in the face of danger,
and our safeguard on life's journey
until you welcome us
to our heavenly home.

Grant this through Christ our Lord.
Amen.

CROSIER
FATHERS AND BROTHERS
National Shrine of St. Odilia
P.O. Box 500 • Onamia, MN 56359
320-532-3103

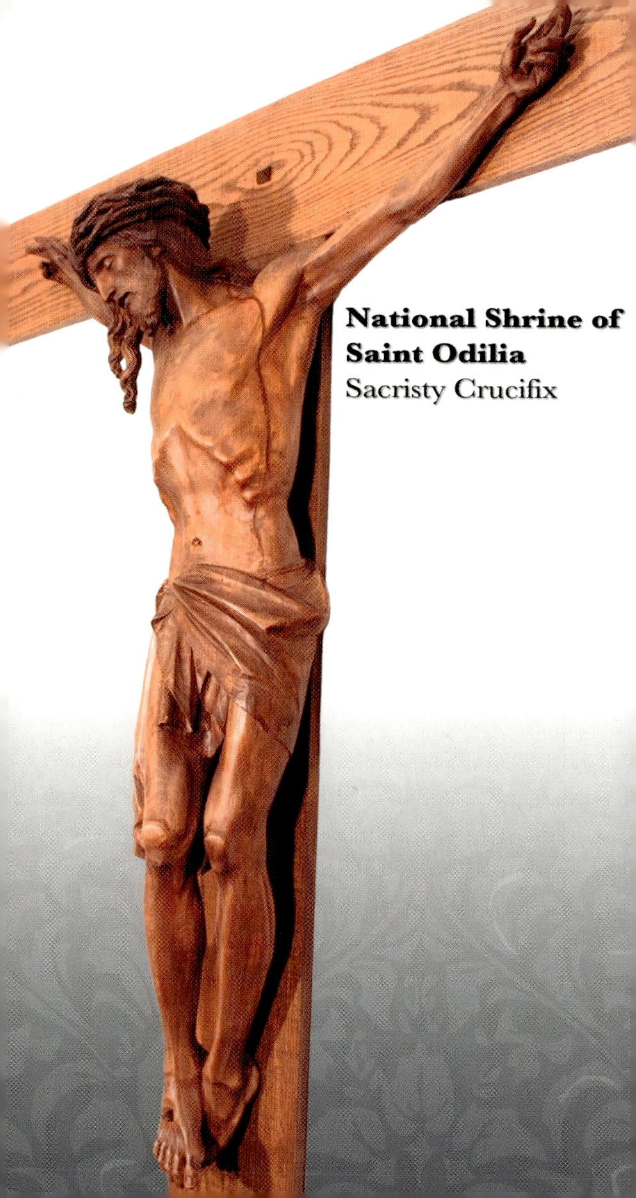

National Shrine of Saint Odilia
Sacristy Crucifix

Map
The Democratic Republic of the Congo Today

Map No. 4007 Rev. 10, July 2011, courtesy of the United Nations. Used with permission.

List of Crosier Missionaries in Congo

Martyrs

The English equivalent is given in parentheses following the confrere's first name; nicknames are enclosed in brackets. Also listed is the place they were assigned in 1964.

Fr. Jef (Joseph) Beckers, osc	Baye
Fr. Rob (Robert) Carremans, osc	Lobi
Fr. Marinus (Marion) Godefrooy, osc	Baye
Fr. Vic (Victor) van Heeswijk, osc	Bondo (Seminary)
Br. Leo (Leonard) Ignoul, osc	Bondo (Mission)
Fr. Gerard Jansen, osc	Bondo (Mission)
Fr. Gerard Kester, osc	Baye
Fr. Godfried Kraewinkels, osc	Bondo (Seminary)
Fr. Paul Kruitwagen, osc	Bondo (Mission)
Fr. Alfons [Fons] (Alphonse) Kuypers, osc	Bondo (Seminary)
Fr. Huub (Hubert) van Lieshout, osc	Lobi
Fr. Jan (John) van Oort, osc	Lobi
Br. Lambert Schoenmakers, osc	Baye
Fr. Hendrik [Rik] (Henry) Snijkers, osc	Bondo (Seminary)
Fr. Albert Timmers, osc	Monga
Fr. Hendrik Verberk, osc	Monga
Fr. Jan (John) Verhoeven, osc	Bondo (Seminary)
Br. Peerke (Peter) Verkuylen, osc	Baye
Fr. Arnold [Nol] Vervoort, osc *assassinated at Dakwa on Nov. 25, 1964*	Dakwa
Fr. Willem (William) Vissers, osc	Bondo (Mission)
Fr. Filip (Philip) Waldram, osc	Monga
Fr. Willem [Wim] (William) van Wetten, osc *assassinated at Dakwa on Nov. 25, 1964*	Dakwa
Br. Jef (Joseph) Wouters, osc	Bili

Bondo Missionaries Not Present on May 30, 1965

Fr. Petro (Peter) Andriessen, osc
died around the time Fr. Verhoeven began his diary, but he is referenced in the text a few times

Fr. Polydoor [Pol] Carremans, osc — Seminary
liberated Nov. 25, 1964

Br. Egbert Mensink, osc — Mission
liberated Nov. 25, 1964

Br. Leonard Rooyakkers, osc — Mission
liberated Nov. 25, 1964

Br. Marcel Smits, osc — Mission
returned from Europe and was on his way back to Buta with Fr. Frans Waldram when heard the news about the massacre

Br. Willem (William) Tieken, osc — Mission
granted furlough; traveled back to Europe in April 1965

Fr. Jan van Wagenberg, osc — Mission
had been ill and was granted furlough; traveled back to Europe with Br. Willem Tieken in April 1965

Fr. Frans Waldram, osc — Seminary
had been in Bangui to get provisions and was trying to get back to Buta when he heard about the massacre

THE HOSTAGES OF MAKONDO

Introduction

The Diocese of Bondo is situated at the northern border of the present Democratic Republic of the Congo,[1] at its center, entirely surrounded by two rivers, the Mbomu and the Uele, suspended almost as if in a hammock. From the east to the west it measures about 466 miles, and from north to south it varies from 62 miles to 124 miles. To the north and to the west of the Mbomu, one finds the Central African Republic with its capital of Bangui. This is the commercial center closest to Bondo, which is reached principally by passing from Monga to Ndu on the border and then to Bangassou, and finally Bangui.

The missionaries at Bangui and that region are Dutch and are of the Congregation of the Holy Spirit. The Crosiers had numerous contacts with them throughout the years.

The southern border of the diocese is also a natural border: the Uele River with its numerous rapids and falls, its elbows, and its islands that are at times almost a mile long. On the other side of the Uele River is the Diocese of Buta. According to the estimations made around 1965, the Diocese of Bondo had about 180,000 people, principally of the Azande tribe. It's only as one goes west, in the vicinity of the mission post of Monga, that one finds another tribe called Mongwandi, the majority of whom live to the west of the Diocese of Bondo, and then to the north, west, and south of Yakoma. The principal commercial products of the region are cotton, palm oil, and coffee.[2] At the town of Baye is a gold mine.

When the Crosier Fathers and Brothers arrived in Bondo in 1920, the present territory of the diocese belonged to the apostolic prefecture of Uele-west (Buta). It was separated in 1926 for the establishment of the apostolic prefecture of Bondo (Uele-northwest),

1 The former Zaïre, and before that the Belgian Congo.

2 Once a thriving industry, this no longer exists.

of which Monsignor Konings, osc, was the first prefect. Under the prefecture of his successor, Monsignor M. Blessing, osc, in 1937, Bondo became an Apostolic Vicariate (and Blessing was ordained a bishop). These were the steps at the time for becoming a diocese with a bishop. With the decision to establish the ecclesial hierarchy of the Congo, Bondo became an independent diocese in 1959. In 1955, Monsignor Adreas Creemers, osc, became the bishop, and at that time there were about fifteen Congolese diocesan priests. Since that time there have been three Congolese bishops, none of them Crosiers.[3] Soon after their arrival, the Crosiers began to look for collaborators in the fields of education and medicine. In 1923 the Sisters of the Heart of Mary of Berlaar, Belgium, came, followed in 1932 by the Ursuline Sisters of the Diocese of Liège in Belgium. These two congregations took care of the teaching of girls. The Berlaar sisters took care of Bondo, Baye, Monga, and Lobi (this was done in collaboration with the Congregation of Congolese sisters founded by them), and the Ursulines took care of the eastern part of the diocese—the posts of Ango, Bili, and Dakwa. What didn't they do? They also took charge of general hospitals; maternity hospitals; clinics; and, in certain parts, lepers' camps!

From 1927 on, the diocese was helped immensely with the coming of the Brothers of Saint Gabriel who took charge of the education of grade-school teachers in a "normal school," as such schools were called in that period. Besides this work, the brothers also took charge of the boys' primary schools at Bondo, Baye, and Ango, as well as alphabetization classes for youth and adults, and also some trade schools. Elementary education in the whole diocese owes it to them that it achieved such a high level. In later years, the Brothers of Saint Gabriel received some Congolese men into their congregation.

In 1964, the Diocese of Bondo had around 60,000 Catholics, or about one-third of the population. The diocesan priests served the parishes of Ndukula, Basende, Mbuma, Bili, Bangoi, and Api, while the Crosiers served at Bondo, Lobi, Monga, Baye, Ango, and Dakwa. The Crosiers also had the direction of the diocesan minor seminary in Bondo. With high hopes for the results, in 1963 the Crosiers added

3 At the time of this English translation a new bishop has recently been appointed whose name is Bishop Etienne (Stephen) Ung'eyowun Bediwegi.

a high school, named "le College" in the European fashion.

Brothers Egbert Mensink, osc; Leo Ignoul; osc; and Marcel Smits, osc, took care of training "mechanics" at the "garage" of Bondo; the same thing took place at Baye under the direction of Father Jan Vanderwegen, osc. This mission post also had a printing press under the direction of Father Marinus Godefrooy, osc, who took orders (for example, for textbooks developed for the schools of Bondo) from beyond the borders of the diocese.

Each mission post had its trade school, of which the principal ones were that of Baye, as already noted (under the direction of the Brothers of Saint Gabriel) and that of Father Petro Andriessen, osc, at Bondo, where there was wood and metal working; mechanics of all sorts; and radio, watch, and bicycle repair.

The agricultural school at Bondo was (and had been for a number of years) directed by a Congolese diocesan priest, who was also the unofficial "Bondo news reporter."

Bondo was on the path of the so-called trans-African highway, which entered the Congo Republic at Bangassou, continued toward the southeast passing by Bondo, and then continued to Buta and Stanleyville (the present Kisangani). At Bondo, it was necessary to cross the Uele by a motorized ferry.

Not far from where one got off the ferry, one could see the official government buildings of the Territory, called "le Territoire."[4] It was a group of official-looking buildings that housed the police and other government offices of the Territory.

Beginning at the Territory and proceeding inland from the river was the only street, which was a little less than a mile long. Here there were stores, of which the majority in those days were owned by Portuguese or Indian merchants, and which were frequented by the local inhabitants. At the end of the street was the "mission." This consisted of a whole group of buildings among which were the cathedral; the mission house, which contained rooms for the Crosier community serving the cathedral; and its many mission stations. The bishop had his own house with living space and offices. Then there was the large minor seminary, the boys' high school ("le College"), the community house of the Brothers of Saint Gabriel (with its

4 Called in this translation the Territory.

The cathedral in Bondo pictured in the 1960s. (Photo courtesy of the Crosier Province of Blessed Theodore de Celles, Europe.)

school, chapel, and annexes), the convent of the Heart of Mary Sisters of Berlaar (with their chapel, schools, boarding school, etc.), the hospital and the maternity hospital, the trade school, the mechanics' garage, and so forth.

You could leave Bondo by any of three routes: to the south in the direction of Buta, to the northeast in the direction of Monga or Baye, and toward the east in the direction of Bili. At the entry of these last two mentioned routes, one crossed over the routes that crossed the main street, which began the part inhabited by the natives, called "la cité" or "le belge."

In Bondo, the so-called missionary personnel lived in four distinct communities: the mission, the seminary, the Brothers of Saint Gabriel, and the Sisters of the Heart of Mary. Each community had its own administration; took care of its own affairs; and had its own kitchen, where there were Congolese cooks who worked under the direction of one of the members of the community.

At the end of August 1964, while some were in Europe on vacation, sick leave, or other business, these others were at their posts working at their noble apostolate. We name them here to give glory to God:

At the mission—Crosier Fathers Jan van Wagenberg, Willem Vissers, Gerard Jansen, and Paul Kruitwagen and Brothers Egbert Mensink, Willem Tieken, Leonard Rooyakkers, Leo Ignoul, and Marcel Smits.

At the seminary—Crosier Fathers Pol Carremans, Godfried

Kraewinkels, Alfons Kuypers, Frans Waldram, Vic van Heeswijk, Rik Snijkers, and Jan Verhoeven.

At the Brothers of Saint Gabriel—Brothers Laurent Bosmans, Leonard van Loon, Bernard de Kegel, Gilbert Asselman, and Hubert Jacobs and two of their Congolese Brothers, Henri Merci and Pierre Bangakya.

At the Sisters of Berlaar—Sisters Assisia, Fredegonde, Eveline, and Paula.

Sometime afterwards, the following religious joined the big community of Bondo coming in from their posts in other parts of the diocese: from the Crosiers at Baye came Fathers Marinus Godefrooy, Gerard Kester, and Jef Beckers and Brothers Peerke Verkuylen and Lambert Schoenmakers; from the Crosiers at Lobi came Fathers Rob Carremans, Jan van Oort, and Huub van Lieshout; from the Crosiers at Monga came Fathers Filip Waldram, Hendrik Verberk, and Albert Timmers. From the Brothers of Saint Gabriel at Baye came Stanislaus Verschueren and Guido de Zwaef and Berlaar Sisters Euphrasie and Ennodia. Some of the Berlaar sisters from Buta also came: Alberta, Narcissa, Giovanna, Hildeberta, and Macrina. Finally, three Capuchin fathers came from Yakoma: Monulf Schrijvers, Leopold Neyens, and Adriaan van den Broucke.

The diary of Crosier Father Jan Verhoeven was delivered to us in two installments. The first installment (covering from August 4, 1964, to December 16, 1964) was brought by Brother Marcel Smits, osc, when he returned to Europe in February 1965. The second installment (which covers the period from December 1964 to May 17, 1965) was given to Father Frans Waldram, osc, when he was released the second time to go to nearby Bangui, in the Central African Republic, to buy some food and medicine for the missionaries. It is probable that the author continued his diary until May 29, when the hostages were put in prison; however, these pages have disappeared. Fortunately we can conclude with two other accounts of the last days. The first is by the Crosier Brother Lambert Schoenmakers, osc, which covers May 24–28, and the second is a report of the last events at Buta (on May 30) as given by Sister M. Eveline of Berlaar after her liberation and return to Belgium.

The notes of Jan Verhoeven and Lambert Schoenmakers were

reworked, all the while trying to respect the original text. The authors themselves would have done the same thing, except that the opportunity was not to be given to them. Their texts came to us without any corrections. We have added a few explanatory notes.

Father Jan Bierens, osc
Father M. Colson, osc

PART ONE

Danger in Bondo

Thursday, August 6, 1964

Since last Monday, the atmosphere in Bondo had been very tense. There are contradictory messages circulating on the subject of Stanleyville. The tension and the jokes about a departure are growing.

Because of their small number, the fathers from the minor seminary are eating at the mission. (Three missionaries were on vacation in Belgium, and two, Father Fons Kuypers and Father Rik Snijkers, were at Bili for the summer.)

In the middle of supper, a Greek businessman from Buta suddenly appears in the dining room: the depot of ammunitions at Buta has been blown up. In polished French, he explains that a great panic reigns and that morale has reached the zero point. Right now there are three families at the door seeking something to eat and a place to stay for the night. Some are put up at the Brothers of Saint Gabriel; the others are given shelter at the minor seminary. This necessitates moving some beds around. The days which follow will be very busy! "Everyone in Buta is fleeing," say the Greeks, "Everybody is headed towards Bondo."

Friday, August 7

The first sisters, brothers, and fathers arrive at various times during the day. There is panic among certain groups of sisters. The Marist Brothers of Buta also give the impression of anxiety. Their provincial, who was making a tour of the Congo, suddenly disappeared a few days ago, without leaving a trace. The Norbertines[5] of the Diocese of Buta were on their annual retreat with Father (Paul) Kruitwagen, osc, when wild happenings disrupted their holy

5 The Order of Canons Regular of Prémontré, hereafter called Premonstratensians.

Fr. Jan Verhoeven, osc
(32 years old)

Fr. Willem Vissers, osc
(56 years old)

Fr. Paul Kruitwagen, osc
(52 years old)

The pictures of the 23 Crosier martyrs appear throughout this section. The age under each name is his age at the time of his death. All portraits of the martyrs are courtesy of the Crosier Province of Blessed Theodore de Celles, Europe.

solitude...[6] The retreat was taking place at Titule, and it's from there that they fled. For this reason they lost all that they had.

They informed us of what transpired on their journey: while the procession of sisters, brothers, and fathers was on its way to Bondo via Titule, Api, and Bili, the ten-ton trucks of the Greeks followed. Precisely because of them, the nocturnal passing of Api would be more difficult. In the middle of the night they passed hours and hours talking while waiting at the ferryboat, at which time certain other individuals decided to make off with their suitcases and disappeared with their booty into the bush. The presence of a policeman prevented this. Then it happened that someone higher in rank than the policeman made it known that the authorities of Buta had taken flight and each one had taken care of his baggage; why couldn't these whites do the same?

Most of this group arrived here late during the night from Thursday to Friday, exhausted from fatigue and hunger. Confusion grew. Those fleeing didn't know whether to continue on to Monga and Bangassou or to stay here.

Some Greeks, who wanted to continue, are retained here. Some sisters and a father who is ill have been authorized to cross the border. Women and children also. The Greeks as well. But, in this case, they are obliged to leave their trucks behind. These measures are understandable: their ten-ton trucks are crammed with all sorts of things; to pass the border under these conditions would be like smuggling goods. So the trucks are staying here, and the men and some women are lodging in some dormitories at the seminary.

During the night of Friday to Saturday some more trucks and automobiles arrive, transporting some Greeks and African authorities from Buta to Likati. Father Frans Waldram left to drive the sisters to Monga-Bangassou. Towards ten o'clock at night, all is calm.

Saturday, August 8

Some Premonstratensians arrive yet around noon, among them are those of Aketi. They divide up between the seminary and the

6 The ellipses in the text appear in the 1965 manuscript. They are not indications that text has been omitted.

mission. At the seminary at noon, there are fourteen people at table. These are principally the younger Premonstratensians who are with us. During the meal, we speak about a meeting that a propagandist for Lumumba held in Bondo.[7] Here, we hadn't noticed anything.

After the meal, the young superior of the Premonstratensians comes to join us and he authorizes the fathers from Aketi to return there on their own responsibility.

All of them, except one brother, leave after the meal. After the siesta, everything is quiet: a normal Saturday afternoon. The Greeks are playing cards close to the dormitory. I can hear the clatter of the glasses and beer bottles. Brother Leo Ignoul and Father Snijkers come back from Bili about three o'clock. Father Fons Kuypers stayed there.

Sunday, August 9

After dinner, some Premonstratensians, coming from Balele (an agglomeration of villages) near Zobia, arrive in Bondo. They speak of tension taking hold of everybody. It seems that there is no real authority left anywhere!

After greeting them, we learn that some fathers have continued their journey to Baye. The sisters of Baye have come to Bondo and the Marist Brothers of Buta have gone to Baye. Father Frans Waldram should be back from Monga already, but we hear that the ferryboat has been destroyed. All this going and coming only makes the tension grow. At the seminary, the atmosphere is still good. Today we played ping-pong again. The Greeks are staying close to their dormitory; they are afraid and say that they want to leave.

After siesta, the usual football[8] game did not take place, but rather Fathers Rik Snijkers and Vic van Heeswijk and I got on our motorcycles and took a tour of Bondo. Everything was peaceful. Afterwards we went over to the sisters' convent where there are still two sisters of Bondo who have now been reinforced with some sisters from Buta.

At the exact moment when we arrived home, the Greeks were taking off on their motorcycles: they are very afraid and cannot stand it. We hope that they don't come back. In the meantime, Father

7 Patrice Lumumba was the prime minister and seemed to be promoting communism.

8 Football in this text is American soccer.

Waldram returns. The sisters have already gone over the border. The ferryboat at Lobi has been destroyed; they made a detour by Dongobe. At Monga everything was calm.

Monday, August 10

After a calm night, the first news that greets us on awaking is that neither the sisters nor the Marist brothers were able to get to Baye. Only a pickup truck got through. After Mass I make a tour of Bondo on motorcycle. Everything is peaceful. The market is already open. The natives give me a friendly greeting except for a young man whose face looked like he was going to a funeral. He probably had a bad night's sleep…

About nine thirty in the morning: Father Rik Snijkers has to go to get the papers and passports of the sisters. The sisters are again in Bondo, but their papers are in the car, which was able to cross the border. So, the sisters are in Bondo and their papers are in Baye. Father Rik is going to get the papers for the sisters because they want to flee yet towards Monga. Why don't they calm down a little?

In the meantime, some soldiers arrive in Bondo from Stanleyville: they are deserters of the A.N.C. (Congolese National Army) and want to go home to mama…

At noon: Father Snijkers and some others who wanted to go to Baye are back; they were not able to cross the river by ferryboat despite the authorization that they had. Apparently the chief of the region has paid the boatmen off so that they won't let anyone pass. The papers of the sisters can yet be salvaged by mail since Father Rik was able to send on a letter while there.

This evening: Tonight at three o'clock the sisters will depart for Monga. I took my mail over for them around nine o'clock. Late in the evening we heard that the sisters won't depart until the morning. In the meantime the question has arisen whether Father Willem Vissers, who is ill, should leave with them.

Tuesday, August 11

About eight o'clock: It is not yet certain that Father Vissers will accompany the sisters to Bangassou. I make the rounds of "la cité" (literally "the town;" however, in context it means the part of Bondo where the natives lived. It is quite large in contrast to the mission and government posts.). Everybody seems to be going about their business as usual. Everybody is friendly.

At eleven o'clock: The sisters still haven't departed. They are saying also that the radio has communicated that there are a lot of corpses lying around Bondo…Among the Premonstratensians there is no unity: some want to return to their missions; others want to go on to Bangassou and even return to Europe. Fathers (Jan) van Wagenberg and Vic van Heeswijk buy the furniture belonging to the C.V.C.,[9] which is leaving Bondo and has put everything on sale. The sisters will depart yet today.

Wednesday, August 12

Today we simply enjoyed playing some football with people who were around. Father Hacken came in from Monga. There also, panic reigns. The women at the Protestant mission would like to depart, but their husbands are still in Stanleyville. The Premonstratensians are still here. When will they return home? In the meantime, we have learned that the sisters have passed the border.

The superior of the Premonstratensians had a conversation with Father van Wagenberg on what to do. They decided to stay here at Bondo for the time being.

In the evening: Radio Bangui gave an excellent detailed report on what is going on here.

Thursday, August 13

About eight o'clock: Father Vissers departs in the Mercedes of Bishop Creemers. The sisters accompany him.

In the afternoon: A Premonstratensian brother departs for Bangassou.

Friday, August 14

I go as assistant to the Sacred Heart Chapel with the pastor, Father Kruitwagen.

No change in the situation. Everything seems calm.

---

9 *Compagnie des Chemins de Fer Vicinaux du Congo* (railroad company)

Fr. Vic van Heeswijk, osc
(37 years old)

Br. Leo Ignoul, osc
(57 years old)

Fr. Rik Snijkers, osc
(37 years old)

The evening: A terrible thunderstorm with high winds surprises us; we owe it to our black chauffeur to get us back in time from our journey.

Saturday, August 15

There's gossip going around that we, the fathers, are hiding out a black businessman. They are looking for him all over! The political parties are beginning to show themselves. Today you could register as a member of the M.N.C. – Lumumba (Communist) party. The opposition party is RADECO.[10]

About noon: Two fathers who had decided to pass over the border come back from Monga. It made us laugh a lot.

Sunday, August 16

A peaceful Sunday, as Bondo has already known thousands of them.

Monday, August 17

According to the radio, it's bad news in Stanleyville.

At the end of the day, Father Snijkers and I go, as usual, for a walk around in order to learn a bit more of Lingala (the local national language). Earlier in the day we had already seen a military truck marauding around. The soldiers said that they were on patrol. When we went to "la cité" there was a crowd that seemed very interested in something. Their faces showed both curiosity and fear. We encountered a few drunk policemen. Trucks were driving around. There were some soldiers walking who were very friendly with us. So what's going on? Suddenly we found ourselves among soldiers who were invading houses all over the place. They seemed to be looking for certain people. We suddenly ran into the director of the primary school astride his bicycle. Gasping for air he told us: "Fathers, don't stay here; return to the seminary. It's not sure that you are safe here." We go back. We find the other fathers who have other news: the M.N.C. (the Lumumba Communist Party) is proceeding to arrest a good number of people. The tension is high. There was a meeting of the M.N.C. going on. People are saying that Bondo is going to

10 *Rassemblement Democratique Congolais* (Congolese Democratic Assembly)

fall under their dictatorship in a few days' time. Our hired workers disappeared as night fell.

At seven o'clock: We're listening to one of Beethoven's symphonies. Our listening is interrupted by some black police who come with a search warrant: they go searching in all our bedrooms, the chapel, and the whole seminary for blacks on the run (probably members of the RADECO party). Morale is falling. The commander himself was nevertheless very friendly. During evening recreation, the beer picks us up. If things continue like this, then we might get through this alright.

During the night, we can hear trucks driving all around.

Tuesday, August 18

In the morning, the cook, without batting an eyelid, recounted how they were searching throughout the night with a great deal of noise for all the members of RADECO. He had no more than just finished when a car stopped before the dining room and the cook was called out to talk to the police. Without a doubt, they were quizzing him to see if we were hiding people for whom he had to prepare meals.

At nine o'clock: Requiem Mass is celebrated for Father Petro Andriessen. Because of the tense situation, we aren't expecting a lot of people.

After Mass: Contrary to every expectation, there were a fair amount of people in church. Some members of the government administration and the white businessmen were there. At our house afterward, they cornered the cook and gave him a good quizzing on the activities of last night.

Brother Peerke Verkuylen of Baye is occupied speaking when Father van Heeswijk comes in with the news that "they" beat up a white man and broke into the house of another and demanded ten thousand francs from each one. It isn't normal that the whites begin to fear.

At the end of the afternoon: I made another tour of Bondo. Everything seems calm.

In the evening: It seems that more and more people are being put into prison. News by radio: Chinese planes have landed in

Stanleyville. That seems a bit dangerous.

Wednesday, August 19

The local officials' meeting took place as normal. The radio announced the assassination of Mulele![11] The two Premonstratensian fathers who had been occupying a post on the other side of the Uele came back to this side. An indescribable fear has taken hold on the other side.

One hears of enormous difficulties at Aketi. A host of rumors make the rounds. You can't verify a thing.

During our evening walk around town, we hear that "he" is coming tomorrow. When we ask who "he" is, nobody knows his name.

Thursday, August 20

It seems that "he" has arrived. About nine thirty in the morning, I made a tour of Bondo by motorcycle. Several main streets were lined with flags. Somebody was coming from Aketi. A lot of people were going down to the M.N.C. building. Some had flowers, others branches of trees. The women were wearing flowers in their hair. Everybody was friendly.

A strange situation. It's almost eleven o'clock, beautiful outside after the threat of rain has passed.

In the evening: "He" hadn't shown up. Some say that "he" is Mulele. He's supposed to come on Saturday.

We are beginning to wonder when the school year is going to start. If the situation doesn't improve, our confreres and lay teachers who are in Europe will certainly not return.

The situation is very strange.

There are bizarre reports going around on the subject of the Congolese Bishop of Buta, Monsignor Jacques Mbali. He will be in a lot of trouble and maybe even assassinated. Some are saying also that when "he" comes, a people's court will be set up to judge all those who are now in prison. Certain ones will be condemned to death.

In the meantime Father Vissers came back from Bangassou,

11 Mulele is the founder of the Simba movement, and the Simba were sometimes called "Mulelists."

healed but still pale faced. Father Frans Waldram was also back with a lot of news from Monga and its surroundings. Some soldiers close to Yakoma had deserted. Father Frans and others had a lot of difficulties in trying to get to Bangassou. He brought two sisters back from Monga. They want to rejoin their post at Titule. This evening we enjoyed some Charlie Chaplin films. The laughter breathes a little courage into us.

Friday, August 21

Around nine thirty: The workers of Brother Leonard (Rooyakkers) and the seminary leave us. They are going to the Territory. It seems that "he" has arrived. Everybody is going down there. You can't see even a stray cat around. They say that the prisoners are lined up before the Territory office in the sun and that they are being judged. Everybody is to show up to demonstrate their allegiance.

At quarter to eleven: The barometer is falling fast…Some of our servant boys have come back white, or rather gray, from fear. They're stuttering from fear. It's unbelievable. It's about men being beat up, thrown into sacks, and then assassinated.

There's other news that arrives: Brother Leo's truck and Father van Wagenberg's Land Rover are requisitioned. "They" will bring them back. The truck's destination is Aketi; the Land Rover will be used for tours of inspection around town and elsewhere. The soldiers tell us fathers that we shouldn't be afraid. If somebody comes to give us trouble at the mission, they assure us that they will shoot the troublemakers right then and there.

The present situation has really turned rotten. Happily, we see our cook come back.

We learn a little later that another car was requisitioned at the sisters.'

At dinner: The ambiance has fallen to zero. Father Paul Meyfroot, superior of the Premonstratensians, has gone to the Protestant mission with Father Paul Kruitwagen. There they find more bad news: a lot of people have been assassinated at Buta.

After siesta: Father Kuypers and Brother Linus van Dijk come back from Bili. Down there everything seems calm for the moment.

Here, the tension is growing. Around five o'clock, a truck full of excited youth pass in front of the seminary. A little later, Father Frans Waldram has something to be frightened about: a car arrives and somebody sticks a rifle out the window, and a clock maker, who was being sent back, jumps out of the vehicle. Happily, it all went peacefully.

After supper: Except for the noise made by trucks on patrol, everything is peaceful. We watch a Charlie Chaplin film.

Saturday, August 22

About eight o'clock: We had spent a calm night. We hear that a part of the prisoners have been liberated, but they have to return tomorrow. I make tour of Bondo. Altogether, it seems rather peaceful.

At eleven o'clock: We begin to endure some very ugly affairs. During dinner, a car suddenly pulls up and stops in front of the dining room. Four soldiers get out. Father Kuypers, who is just coming from his room to the dining room, is threatened by one of them with a pistol. The soldier fires once into the ground. He then comes into the dining room crying out: "What is this? Everybody to the Territory!" We had to go out single file. They want an amplifier. We assure them that we don't have one. When they say again that we must get down to the Territory, we ask if we can finish our dinner. They permit us to do so. We quickly finish our meal and get ourselves down there by foot. Everywhere, we meet people who pull back as we come through. The other fathers from the mission are also coming. I don't see the brothers. We come up to the office. There are already a mass of people present. We are the last ones to arrive. They scream that we should run very fast. We do it. All the people present are carrying flowers or branches of trees.

And then the People's Court sits down. We, the fathers, are lined up two by two. Right in front of us are the other whites. There's singing and a lot of discussion. As far as we are concerned, we're told that the children at our schools no longer should pay their tuition. We are lined up directly in front of the building. At a certain moment, we are told to turn around. There, under a flag, two men are standing straight, hands tied. They are badly treated. They are going to be killed. One of them is a government minister from Paulis, vice president of the Province of Uele and the minister of finance. We know him very well; he comes from Monga and has already given money to the school. They go toward them with their machine guns and kill them. Horrible! I have never seen men gunned down and especially in this fashion: they are transformed into sieves.

They fall, agitated by convulsions, and then they are lying on the grass full of blood.

We have to turn around again, and some young women have to march up to one of the Territory buildings with a key. They carry out all the papers and tear them up. Two policemen of Bondo are roughed up. A frightening spectacle: four soldiers are the masters of Bondo and kill two men in public.

The four soldiers armed with rifles ask the people for their opinion. Even the fathers are asked to respond or to sing with the crowd. Suddenly, somebody finds in a book the photo of Father Hulskamp.[12] One of the Premonstratensians resembles him. He is made to come out of the ranks, and the soldiers propose to kill him. We tell them that he is not Father Hulskamp. They leave him alone, and he returns to the ranks.

Suddenly, the people begin to murmur. They point to one of the bodies: "He's not dead, he's getting up." Actually, one of the victims was pushing himself up a bit, slowly, on an elbow. The soldiers want to fire, but the people say, "He's not a bad man. The fact that he's not dead is proof!" They call a truck. They literally "throw" the man on the truck and take him to the hospital. After some songs, we are permitted to go home. We are broken in spirit, numb with terror.

About eleven o'clock, a man appears in the recreation room to tell us that one of us should transport the wounded man in a car to Monga so that he can be cared for by a doctor. Two of the Premonstratensians, Father Paul Meyfroot and Brother Joost Sleeckx, depart immediately in their Mercedes. Sister Paula tells us that this trip is for nothing: the unfortunate man has seventeen bullets in him. At the hospital he was conscious; he went to confession and received the last sacraments. He was very peaceful.

After the siesta: We ate hardly a thing in the dining room and spoke less. Nobody rested. During the siesta we could hear "youth"

12 A Crosier Father assigned to the Congo but in Europe for an illness.

Fr. Godfried Kraewinkels, osc (43 years old)

Fr. Filip Waldram, osc (55 years old)

Fr. Fons Kuypers, osc (40 years old)

passing by the seminary in a truck and singing. Around three o'clock they came looking for the Mercedes of Bishop Creemers. Brother Marcel came over to warn us. During the morning, during the execution, it seems someone came to look for the Mercedes and also Brother Leo, because the ferryboat had been demolished. They told the brothers: "If you don't repair the ferryboat immediately, we will kill you!" So they worked on it until three o'clock.

During tea time, some members of the "youth" arrive in a car of Comaco[13] and requisition our little Volkswagen. Now we have nothing.

At quarter to six: Fathers Paul Meyfroot and Brother Joost have returned. The man died thirty miles from Bondo. They had continued on to Lobi and heard that Father Huub van Lieshout had passed some thrilling hours. When they came, he was all alone. The attack was as complete as it was sudden. They stole money, radios, and tape recorders. One door, for which he had no key, was forced open by shooting out the lock.

In the evening: They are passing regularly by the seminary. They come to stock up on beer at our place! From what we heard afterward, they took the whiskey that the brothers had, and at the mission they took two bottles of wine. We are going to bed early. It's calm now, so most of us pass a peaceful night.

Sunday, August 23

The morning: During morning Mass at the sisters' house, at the moment of the consecration, a soldier suddenly appeared in the sanctuary to say that they will be back in a little while to take a cow.

During breakfast, we learn that the Mercedes of the Premonstratensians has also been requisitioned. We eat little and get on our way to the High Mass at the Cathedral. During Mass, we can still hear vehicles going around outside, but for the rest it's peaceful. The people say nonetheless that they haven't departed as yet: now and then somebody is killed.

At eleven thirty: It's a beautiful summer day. It's peaceful; you can't hear anything. We're going to play ping-pong. Some tension again. Father Polydoor Carremans is here with his money. It's a lot of

13 *Compagnie Commerciale Agricole du Congo*—a company that promoted the growing of cotton and palm oil and then exported its products.

money for the salaries of the teachers. We hide it.

A passing word: our personnel are wonderful. They come to work as much as is possible; they're nervous, but courageous. One of them told us: If we are going to die, we will die all together, we with you. That is the same kind of calm resignation that touched us at the executions.

After siesta: A good nap. They have certainly left. What a relief. Everybody can feel it. Except for not having any beer to drink, for the most part we're eating normally since yesterday. While listening to the radio, I hear a recording of combat in the streets of Bukavu. That puts you completely back into the mood of the day before yesterday.

After Benediction: The mood is fallen a little. On leaving the church, we see our car followed by another loaded with members of "The Youth." They are saying that one of the four soldiers has remained here, whereas the others have indeed departed. For the rest, it's a calm evening. We hear later that they have thrown a body of one of the victims into the Uele.

In the evening: In observing certain confreres you can see that they are under a certain tension. Late in the afternoon, we honor the games of society; among others, we play cards. One tries to forget. The sisters' cow is still waiting for the soldiers.

At evening recreation, we play cards again, this time two tables full. We are trying to keep up the ambiance. The last ones go to bed around midnight. Everything is peaceful.

Monday, August 24

In the morning: I heard at the brothers'[14] that four truckloads of soldiers have arrived and that there will be "some special events" again at the Territory.

At nine o'clock, everything is quiet, but everybody is tensed up, especially since, during breakfast, our workers came and said that they didn't dare stay and that they would go home. We ate little at breakfast. A little later, some soldiers arrive to charge their batteries. I am the first one to see them. Father Frans Waldram, whose job this is, is at the mission. I go to get him. A search has just begun at the mission. I am really fearful when I see the soldiers with their

14 Fr. Verhoeven often celebrated morning Mass in the chapel of the Brothers of Saint Gabriel.

crazy attitudes. I see that Brother Egbert has some difficulties: he is dressed like a civilian and does not have a beard. One of the soldiers is particularly brutal. The rest aren't too bad. Father Frans Waldram and I receive authorization to return to the seminary. We quickly warn everybody that "they" are going to arrive. We had just finished our task, and there "they" are. There are six of them armed with rifles of the type that the police use. One of them, dressed like a civilian, has an old rusty rifle that he found in the workshop of Father Andriessen. They brought the Belgian flag along from the mission. They left the papal flag there. While they are occupied in the room of Father (Godfried) Kraewinkels, one of them comes out and notices us, Father Kuypers and myself. We are running a bit too quickly in his opinion. From being a bit jovial, he now turns against us and decides to search all of our rooms for I don't know what. On the other hand, the other soldiers were different. Some seemed rather dull. In the rooms of Fathers Frans Waldram and Theo Hacken they had to listen to the audiotapes to see that there was nothing political on them. In an empty room, they find some flowerpots made from the sockets of mortar shells from the end of the Second World War. We explain it to them. One of them says, "And where is your cannon?" Another soldier realizes that this is a ridiculous question and proceeds to another room. After our rooms, they want to see the carpenter shop and then the kitchen. When they realize that the workers are not here, they give the order to call them back immediately. They say if they do not come back, they will be killed.

During all this time, the little but courageous diocesan priest, Father Jean (John) Mange, stays at the soldiers' sides and accompanies them from door to door. They are not allowed to touch or to take anything. If they want something, he has to take it first and put it on the floor, after which they gather up everything. There can be no direct relations between them and us.

To our great relief, they leave after half an hour. The tension is always more serious than the events themselves. The soldiers tell Father Jan van Wagenberg that the fathers of Buta should return to their mission.

Brother Leonard learns that the soldiers were not happy that the brothers and sisters were not present for the execution.

At eleven thirty: Everything is quiet again. Some of the workers have come back. Father Paul Meyfroot, the superior general of the Premonstratensians, is occupied in peeling the potatoes in the entry of the kitchen. Today we have a drink before dinner: we found ten bottles of Martini[15] in the room of a lay professor; the searches seem to also have an interesting aside to them for us.

After siesta: At noon, we ate some pies with whipped cream on top. They were great! After that, some found that they could sleep a bit, others of us not. It is almost one o'clock in the afternoon, and we hear some gunfire and some singing far away. They come in search of a battery, and it seems that they are in fact "at work." They're killing people. They're shooting yet. The echo of the shootings invades the seminary on all sides. Trucks pass going every which way.

I learn just now that at noon they gathered the Premonstratensians from the mission. One soldier came to tell them that they had taken flight and that it wasn't a good thing. They should go back to their missions. The commandant spoke to them a second time. So after that, they left. We hear that the victim of a little while ago was the last administrator of Bondo. They also killed a woman.

After supper: Father Filip Waldram, the superior at Monga, has just arrived. The members of the parish council of Monga have accompanied him. The sisters and Father Joe Wagemans left Monga yesterday evening. There are three fathers left. Father Waldram tells us that the horrors that we have seen here happened up there also. Three policemen were at the Territory when the first soldiers arrived. They asked the police to take off their hats, and then they shot them. He also told us about their "magic" idea of war. The cries of "mai-mai" have something to do with the murmur of a lion who is thirsty. In Swahili, "simba" means lion. Mai is also a kind of water with which they are sprinkled, in such a way that they feel invincible. But a simple contact can weaken this invincibility a little. The evening is quiet.

Tuesday, August 25

At quarter of ten: I sit myself down at my typewriter. Some things have already happened today. Where I'm from in Holland,

15 A brand of vermouth

they are celebrating a wedding. My oldest sister is getting married. They don't know anything of what's going on here, even though they certainly aren't tranquil about the situation.

News of this morning: This morning, like I do every morning, I went by motorcycle to the Brothers of Saint Gabriel to celebrate Mass. Immediately after Mass (I still had the amice in my hand), we heard the arrival of a group of noisy soldiers. They have come to seize the cars. There's a lot of noise and brutality. I returned to the chapel to wait.

I hear them depart. The brothers have "fixed up" a car by plunging a spark plug into some filthy oil. Despite that, they leave, even with the motor sputtering. The car ends up on the main route. There, it stops again, exactly at the intersection of the main route and the road that goes between the brothers' and the mission. We watch the spectacle from afar. They try to push it; they demand a chauffeur. This only makes us more upset. I decide to take my meal with the brothers. We eat like starving people. During this time, there is all this squealing at the roadside. After the meal, I return home despite the situation, because the others at the seminary might begin to worry about my absence. There is only one soldier waiting on the side of the car that's not working. He lets me pass in saluting me halfheartedly. At the seminary, I see Brother Leonard: he has a strange look about him. I go up to him and make a remark about how pale faced he looks. "They came to go on a trip, put all the fathers in a truck, and then left." What to do, except to go immediately back to the brothers.' Getting back over there, I spy a truck loaded with whites before the mission of the brothers. They give me a sign to stop, and then I have to come up to the truck on my cycle. I leave my motorcycle and get up into the truck. All the brothers are also within. The truck starts with a great noise. Where is it going?

Heavily slanting from side to side, the truck goes around Bondo: it is filled with the fathers from Buta, all the Crosiers, and the brothers from Bondo. We pass the Territory buildings. We continue on the main route. There's only one possibility: we are on our way to the prison. There we have to descend and to line up two by two. They want to throw us into the small cells. They made the other prisoners vacate. We recognize among them the president of RADECO. They hit them like they were crazy. Then, they take us and march us down to the large "hall." They push us in and then brutally close the door. We try to pay attention as the door is violently opened: Father Hebette has to follow them. He gets up quickly and is gone. The door is closed. It's at this point that we begin to really become afraid. In the corner where I am sitting, it occurs to us that it was in precisely his room that they found the Belgian flag. What are they going to do with him? We are thinking that the others among us who have some authority (for example, those in charge of the money for teachers) will probably undergo the same thing. Somebody begins to pray the rosary. We have prayed a few decades when suddenly there's a cry from the exterior that we should stop praying. The door opens, and a haughty young fellow enters and tells us: "Don't pray loudly, that makes us feel nasty." We continue the prayer in silence. Our morale is very low. We discuss what we will say and what we will keep quiet about.

After not quite an hour, the door opens. We all have to get out. The young fellow of the execution is there again with Monsignor Creemers' car. He is not too mean. The diocesan priest, Father Jean, speaks. They are going to drive us home. They ask for a truck. Some other soldiers arrive. They make the fathers from Buta line up. I don't understand what they are saying. It seems again the question of why they do not return to Buta. We wait and wait. In the prison hall, there are some chairs, which are now offered to the oldest among us. Father Willem Vissers begins to play a native game of a kind of billiards with another confrere. The people at the prison begin to talk to us. They know several of the fathers, and the conversation begins to take on a pleasant note, as if nothing special has happened! A car comes for those who are from Buta. They are stuffed in, piled up in the Peugeot, while another vehicle arrives, a pickup truck, and a group of Crosiers are stuffed in like sardines. Arriving at the mission, we have the joy of seeing Father Hebette. He was a "good" father and now has to return immediately to Buta. It happens that while I am typing at the machine, the fathers from Buta are "transported." It's too bad, because there had developed a real solidarity between us, and we had now been through a lot together. Another thing: it is admirable to note that under such circumstances certain fathers appear like statues that are more than human; they witness to a courage and a calm that one had not believed them capable of. One speaks also of a certain sister who was unbelievably courageous. She works at the hospital and has to put up with a lot! On the other hand, two of the sisters are all nerves and are no longer able to sleep. It happens that Father Filip Waldram might be able to take them to Monga. I am finishing here. We will see.

After siesta: The tension is palpable, unbearable. Brother Marcel says that at the mission there is a continual going and coming of cars. Every three minutes, they come to take a car again or to bring it back. Finally somebody says that they can no longer search for cars. The garage is working overtime because there are so many cars that aren't working.

In the meantime, the soldiers are beginning to steal. They just stole the watch of a Premonstratensian. It's four thirty in the afternoon. This father was in the midst of reading in the recreation room. Another radio has disappeared from the mission.

Father Filip Waldram is still here. He has to await the soldiers who should come back from Ndu.

We have heard that they beat to death a white from Baye. He was the type of old colonist who could never shut up.

At the professional school of Father Petro Andriessen, they are stealing watches like flowers on the side of the road. We learn that the sacristan at the cathedral was upset this morning. He warned the pastor that there were other Belgian flags in the cupboards of the sacristy.

It seems the communiqué that a woman had been killed is false.

Some sisters from Titule, who are not from here, come to see the seminary. They dare. Everything is quiet now. One can see all over groups of fathers standing like schoolchildren on the playground. A very small soldier (some young school kids are sometimes the most accomplished soldiers) comes in to ask for gas and a motorcycle. Father Frans Waldram says that there isn't any. A few yards from there are two motorcycles in the library. On hearing this, I decide that in the future I will go on bicycle to celebrate my Masses.

During supper, the atmosphere is fairly tense. After the meal, we play cards, at two tables. We drink beer (why keep it? They will only come and take it from us.), and we smoke some cigars. All evening it is quiet. Father Filip Waldram is still here. Those from Monga are asking themselves some questions. This evening, the radio from Bangui gives a good report. We deduce that the refugees from Monga have arrived in Bangassou.

Wednesday, August 26

In the morning: I was at the brothers' to celebrate Mass. No problem. A typical fact to note: at breakfast time there is always a certain tension. Is this their hour? Already two times, they came upon us at this time. The Parish Committee of Monga arrived after breakfast, and Father Filip Waldram was able to depart. Everything is quiet. The black sisters from Lobi came with something that will cause a little stir; they came to Bondo with a black businessman.

The gossip is that all the soldiers have departed in the direction of Yakoma. There's probably something going on up there. We haven't heard the final word. Would the National Congolese Army already be there? I just came back from the mission. (It's nine thirty.) There is a car broken down on the route toward Bili. They are accusing Brother Leo of not doing a good job in repairing the car. They're having it pulled back here. A little after, the soldiers arrive anew for an inspection. Enough already! A second group of soldiers arrive who will not permit the search. The reason: They cannot continue to cause these disturbances at the mission. In the meantime we hear that the white who was wounded at Baye will be driven under escort to Bangassou. The children of the businessmen will follow the same route: they have to get back to Belgium in time to begin school. All the workers of Brother Leonard have returned. That gives a sense of peacefulness.

At eleven o'clock: Everything is peaceful. They came to the brothers' house to ask for money. They were able to get rid of them for seven thousand Belgian francs.

At quarter past three: We're not too bothered. Some brat of a kid came to Father Polydoor Carremans to threaten him with a bayonet. Yesterday he stole a watch from us. He wants yet another watch. He didn't receive it. Father Polydoor received the order to open his "armoire." That did it. He was squarely issued the order to go to the

Fr. Huub van Lieshout, osc
(32 years old)

Br. Peerke Verkuylen, osc
(66 years old)

Br. Jef Wouters, osc
(59 years old)

devil, and Father pursued him until he was beyond the property of the seminary.

Around two o'clock, all the workers left again: there will be a People's Court again. We haven't heard any shooting. About four o'clock, Brother Leonard met one of the workers of the brothers. He's an old man without teeth. Leonard asked him why he hadn't gone to the People's Court. The old man's answer came out in a bewildered sort of way: "I am a member of the Youth Group! We have off during the day, because during the night we have to dance and to look for people who are fleeing."

In the meantime, we get the last word on the arrest. Everything is about the Belgian flag that they discovered at the mission. This flag was spread out on the ground between the Territory and the post office, and a truck overflowing with fathers and brothers had to run back and forth over the flag…so Father Hebette was not immediately brought back to the mission because he had to explain in public, before the Territory, the question of the flag. Why did we have a flag? "Bah!" responded Father Hebette, "It's made of good cloth, and you can always make good clothes for the children out of it." This response was accepted.

In the evening: Everything is peaceful. Father Frans Waldram brings out his tape deck during recreation. We drink some beer and play cards, while everything is accompanied by some soft joyful music. When we go to bed, you can hear in different places drums beating and the youth who sing.

Thursday, August 27

At mid-morning: At the brothers' they say that the soldiers have come back from Ndu. It seems that the People's Court will sit again today. At the mission, we hear that during the night the white who was wounded was carried away in the greatest secrecy. It's still calm over at the garage. Let's hope that the brothers who work there will at least have the time to take a breath. At the seminary, we notice how tired the workers are: they had to dance all night again.

After breakfast, everybody looks for a little work to do. Somebody paints a new room, we put together a new arrangement in the library for the periodicals, Father Kuypers keeps busy in the chapel, etc. The soldiers have put a roadblock up at the mission. No one is now allowed to enter. Everything is peaceful this rainy day.

At six thirty: A group of us fathers goes over to the sisters' house. Here we get some more news. Among other things, two little urchins of the Youth who were looking for people in flight during the night came upon a distillery of local liquor. They began to drink. Some soldiers found them and shot them point blank. In their own way, they have an iron discipline. They say that up until now, eleven people have been assassinated. The soldiers are camping on the grounds of Comaco. The urchins who are employed there are occupied day and night with their meals and washing their clothes. As far as sex is concerned, there is a strict abstinence imposed on the soldiers. It seems that it was this way years ago during the tribal wars.

Yesterday, they also killed another who was on their "list." In the last communication we learned that all of them are departing for Stanleyville this evening, even the Youth.

During the course of the evening: someone remarked at supper that this was one of the calmest days since the beginning of the "war." What happened later showed that he spoke too soon. About quarter after eight, we were listening to the radio when we saw the headlights of a car. It was coming our way. They called for Father Godfried Kraewinkels: "Father Fritz, the key to your door." A new search. Soldiers were coming from all over, about fifteen of them. They are always looking for members of RADECO. They came from the mission, and then went by the apartment of the bishop, where they picked up the major piece of the ham radio. And always, there's the same question: "Where is Monsignor? We know he took flight because he belongs to RADECO!" Father van Heeswijk accompanied them again all through the seminary.

Everything went calmly enough. They didn't find our motorcycles or our motorbikes. We all ended up in the recreation room. Here the party began! The commander, with a four-gallon stomach, was drunk and began to mock Father Frans Waldram because his tape deck still was playing music. He was mocking us and then chewing us out. We had to go and get some more beer. Then some wine. The commander did not stop his sermon for one second…it was visibly boring to the soldiers. One of them who was outside with us said: "He's bothering you for no reason." On the inside he continued the monologue of an idiot. After a few threats, they finally left, abandoning all of the drinks.

Evening recreation continued, but very quietly, since we had no energy left. As we went to bed we could hear trucks rolling around and some drumming...Africa dances...on orders!

Friday, August 28, Saint Augustine

I went by foot to celebrate Mass at the brothers.' Everything is calm at their place. "They" didn't come last night. During breakfast there were moments of *silentium magnum* (great silence): what will happen today?

At quarter to nine: A woman who is a grade-school teacher in Baye comes to the seminary. She has an anxious look and is afraid. We huddle around to get the news. After greetings she begins to murmur in a frightened tone: "The fathers in Baye send greetings. Nothing serious has happened to them. When the soldiers came they had to arrange themselves in order on the outside, but nothing else happened!" Baye is okay then. But Monga, Bili, Ango, Dakwa, and Lobi? This incertitude is really frightening.

I come to learn that Father Vissers went down to the Territory with diocesan priest Father Jean in order to discuss all this affair of last night.

At quarter past ten: The barometer goes up! Father Vissers and Father Jean come back from their "palabres"[16] at the Territory. The commander was departing for Aketi. He received them in a friendly manner. They explained everything to him and made up a list of things that had been stolen.

He apologized for not having the situation entirely under control, the Youth, for example...He asked them if they had yet received back the small motorcycles and was very surprised when the answer was negative. They were brought back in a car, accompanied by guards who are now stationed before the buildings of the mission. Any person who wants to enter without reason is to be shot right on the spot. All of this is comforting to us.

16 A word used all over central Africa to indicate a discussion of all those concerned to resolve a problematic situation. This rather "democratic" procedure exists alongside the authority of the hereditary chiefs of the tribes as well as that of the officials of the government in power.

We know that we cannot take confidence in these illusions; however, even the illusions are comforting for the moment, at least enough to give you a good appetite.

At six in the evening: I just got back from the mission where we are helping with the decoration. The way leading to the hospital is decorated to prepare for the arrival of the great "doctor" of Aketi. This famous doctor, in one way or another, seems to be immune to the bullets of the Simba. Father Vissers told us a good story. After some discussion, diocesan priest Father Jean and Father Vissers were able to leave. Father Vissers went immediately to the brothers to give them the good news of the recent decisions made at the Territory. On arriving, they came upon a dozen soldiers who were "at work." They had a little bit of everything that they were carrying along: radios, tape decks, etc. Father Vissers said to them: "My dear fellows, I have just come from your commander, and he told me that every search and all looting are absolutely forbidden." The head of the group showed a little fear, but they continued and took the batteries of some cars. Father Vissers immediately jumped up on his bike to go warn the two guards at the mission. They immediately arrived, and the others left without taking anything. Another remarkable thing: one of the guys who is in charge of our security and our goods was, no less than two days ago, one of the most enthusiastic looters at the mission!

Saturday, August 29

At ten minutes to nine: Everything is peaceful this morning, and will be so most of the day.

At quarter past six: The library for the periodicals is at last ready! Besides that, there were a few false alerts today. Every time the soldiers arrived it was to recharge some batteries, but each time we had the idea that they had come to look for us, because the general had arrived today.

During tea, some soldiers suddenly appeared in the dining room. They wanted to buy a watch. Nobody wanted to sell them one. It seems that neither the "doctor" nor the general are at Aketi. Others say again that he has already arrived. You can't trust any communication. Two people were killed again today. One was a grade-school teacher who had been let out of jail yesterday, arrested again today, and immediately put in front of the firing squad.

In the meantime, we come to learn some supplementary details on the subject of the disappearance of that white man from Baye. He was secretly taken from the hospital during the night and taken to Monga. At the ferryboat passage at Fakka, the car broke down, and they gathered all the inhabitants of a village on the other side of the river, and they made them push the car all the way to Monga (can you imagine that!). It was about eight miles. They wanted to do everything so that they wouldn't be reproached with the murder of a white man. We notice that more and more the orders from their superiors are very severe on this matter!

At quarter past eight: The surprises continue. I heard at the mission that a Protestant pastor arrived in Bondo. He was returning from home leave in Norway and was able to come to Bondo by way of Leopold-Bumba. That he could get here safe and sound shows us that they cannot harass without a good reason.

After a very quiet evening recreation, we go to bed even as the bad times continue.

Sunday, August 30

After High Mass: The Simba have certainly never heard of the sabbath rest. We gathered this morning at the cathedral about eight thirty. The comedy began again in the churchyard. We see a few soldiers who are marching to the mission for a search. The guards ran away immediately, and after a few cries of "simba-simba-mai-mai," nobody knew what to do. We went into the cathedral. I lifted up the curtain that is behind the altar, and I saw the soldiers in the cathedral. I withdrew. I heard in the church the cry, "Over there, there's a father who's fleeing!" The moment that we got outside some Simba came up to us and asked: "Where is the father who fled?" We shrugged our shoulders. They screamed again: "Let's go, everybody over to the house." Two soldiers come with us, one with a machine gun and the other with two rifles. In silence, we go back to the seminary. The soldiers search some rooms and then go away. We don't understand a thing of what's going on. Everything is probably due to a misunderstanding. The soldiers didn't realize perhaps that it is Sunday. They saw all the fathers together at the cathedral, and this made them afraid. At the seminary we talk a bit with a young man from the high school. He tells us that the soldiers have entirely upset the population. They have to dance all night. If they take a little rest, a truck full of soldiers arrives, and everybody is invited to dance with all kinds of threats. He also said that the most abominable stories are circulating among the people.

A quarter of an hour later, some other soldiers show up for a search. These are probably newly arrived groups who don't yet know the rules. They say: "If we find some rifles here, you will be shot on the spot!" Then, they leave.

At ten thirty: We've just learned something unnerving. Father Willem Vissers had accompanied some soldiers to the dwelling of the bishop; there also they were looking all over for some arms. Father Willem proposed to them to also search the trunks of Monsignor Daniel, our Congolese vicar general who is studying in Europe. Then we would've been finished with this matter. The soldiers were in agreement. However, they found a revolver in the first trunk they opened. After the threats of a little while ago, this is not very comforting.

At seven o'clock: What remained of this Sunday continued in the same way that it had begun: miserably. A little before dinner, they came again to "buy" some radios, clocks, and a flag. This evening, one of them asked again for my watch. I refused, and he did not insist. If he had, I would have given it to him. That wouldn't have been a catastrophe: almost all of us have old watches from the workshop of Father Petro Andriessen.

We hear that they have again harassed the whites. During the night, some soldiers were passing by before the stores (these half-drunk types never sleep!), and they noticed the civil watchmen. They wake the whites up and harangue them that these men have to pass the night outdoors while their masters are in bed! The whites broke down from sheer exhaustion. After that, they could go back to bed.

At eight thirty: Since seven o'clock it's been thundering and lightning, but the storm passes us by. This adds to the ambiance of "a catastrophe." At seven o'clock, we heard a lot of gunfire. Let's hope that there won't be any more cadavers.

Fr. Gerard Jansen, osc
(59 years old)

Br. Lambert Schoenmakers, osc
(47 years old)

Fr. Jef Beckers, osc
(49 years old)

Monday, August 31

The day dawned after a peaceful, but rainy, evening and night: it is truly the Congolese rainy season. By the time I arrive at the brothers' (on foot with boots, raincoat, and umbrella), I am soaked to the bones. The commemorative images of Father Andriessen have arrived from Baye to the brothers' house. The man who had the courage to bring them here suffered for it. He was put in prison. They identified the package and tore up the letter that accompanied it.

At eight thirty: Rain, rain, rain! It's raining buckets! Because of the rifles that they still had in the house, Brother Lawrence Bosmans, the superior of the Brothers of Saint Gabriel, had some tense moments yesterday. They put a machine gun to his chest for five minutes. He was in a state of shock!

At eleven thirty: Father Paul Meyfroot came to see me in my room. We were speaking of original sin when I heard a noise that I missed for a long time: the motorcycle of Father Rik Snijkers. Two soldiers came to get it. They didn't know what to do with it but got it going anyway. The motor coughed and spit. Another motorcycle leaves us. The fourth? Our motor scooters are still hidden in the library, full of patience and hope of better days.

At three o'clock: Couldn't nap. We were just in bed when we heard a violent noise. It appears that the roof over Father Snijkers' room decided to give out, and so several tiles fell onto the ceiling. We had just forgotten this noise when we heard a motorcycle approaching, that of Father Rik! An asthmatic motor, a piston that didn't function anymore, a cable in the clutch that was torn out: there it is, the result of two hours of being abused, a motorcycle that for eight years had been cared for like a baby. A little later I heard Father Rik running his cycle with a soldier riding on back: a lesson in driving…

At quarter past eight: Not much news. At the garage, the brothers had a bad day; they were threatened by two brats who made them repair a motor that will be broken tomorrow. A bad headache for the day.

About five o'clock in the morning, we heard rifle shots.

It's become illegal to listen to the radio, so while someone is listening inside, another keeps watch so that no one comes near or betrays us.

Tuesday, September 1

Just at the moment that I was going over to the brothers', an airplane flew over Bondo. The clouds hid it from sight. What does this "new" event signal for the future of Bondo?

At the brothers' house, they tell me about how one of the Congolese brothers had to "sell" his watch for five hundred francs.

At nine o'clock: All of our workers still come and are remaining faithful. All of them now wear a white badge on which it is mentioned that they are a "worker" or a "boy" at the mission. People are saying that all the Simba are going to Aketi to be immunized or purified by means of their "mai" (witchcraft water).

Meal at noon: The peace of the morning served to make us hungry. As far as having a good siesta goes...we are soon resigned. About twenty after one, a gunshot goes off right near us. I thought it was coming from the carpenter shop. For others it seemed to be coming from another place, but even so, it was rather close.

During the coffee break: Everybody is talking and giving their version of the gunshot at noon. At the mission, all the fathers left their beds; the Simba who were stationed at the mission also heard the shot and thought that something was going on at the mission and they came running and crying out: "So, there are still some rifles here!"

At six o'clock: Finally the mystery of the gunshot at noon is resolved. The soldiers were busy looting the store of a white who had left quite a while ago. They were trying to carry away as much as possible, and they asked the civilians not to knock over anything... This order was not carried out rapidly enough, so one of the Simba fired in the air. Since this happened in the Belgian quarter, we all heard it.

We had all thought for some time that the children of the businessman Lalji had already departed, but, in fact, they didn't leave until yesterday. One of them was able to drive, but they had to come back. Today the school year opened in Europe. When will it start here?

At eight o'clock: This day was a day of rest, at least at the seminary. At the garage, the activity was particularly intense today: the repairing of the Mercedes of the Premonstratensians for which

Brother Marcel received one hundred francs. The fathers at the mission have discovered in the meantime a nice expression for the news: for what seems to be, one should have said, that this or that might have happened…

I hide my radio, but I have the urge to bring it out again. It's so quiet.

Wednesday, September 2

After breakfast: At the brothers', a watch has again been sold for two thousand francs. Yesterday evening a soldier came to the mission to explain his viewpoint on the military situation. He was a grade-school teacher of the diocese of the Premonstratensians (Buta). He was drunk! The bottom line was that everything was the fault of the American communists! He would like to fight with them. The plane that had passed had been one of theirs; it had dropped four bombs, but the Simba had taken hold of them with their bare hands, and in their hands the bombs had turned to water!

They say we will have a free day in order to go look for food for men and beasts.

At ten thirty: And so it continues…a Simba just came and departed with my motor scooter. We now have two left…

After siesta: There is a big rumor going around town: They have again looted and completely emptied a store. Lalji has come back; he had bought some sausage for us.

At quarter past eight: At supper time some Simba came to buy some beer. We have learned that two people have been killed, one of which was a businessman from Buta whom they found here at the market.

Thursday, September 3

After breakfast: In coming back from the brothers', I hear some shots fired. At the mission, where I quickly passed by to take a cup of coffee, they are discussing the last communications on the radio: Coquilhatville will fall, and Stanleyville will not be attacked as yet.

At the seminary two cars were already here before breakfast. One vehicle will depart (finally!) to get some food. A black brother will drive the truck.

At nine thirty: We are hearing an intense firing of weapons. It's nerve-wracking to listen to. This morning a young man arrived here who is a seminarian. He spent several weeks trying to get here. He was imprisoned at Buta and at Aketi. They took all his money and many of his clothes.

At ten thirty: All of a sudden the workers leave and go down to the Territory. Does the sword of Damocles have another threat for us? They're saying that the big chief is going to come...A half-hour later, the workers return. The big chief has not arrived; they will alert them at the proper time.

At noon: We learn from a soldier (these soldier types talk a lot!) that they gave some whites a bad time. They assembled them together, gave them a few punches, and then proceeded to harangue them on the lowering of prices.

After siesta: The mood barometer was low today at dinner. This Monday is rather sad for Father Polydoor Carremans whose feast day it is. We are always hearing gunshots. But about four o'clock, it's peaceful again.

At quarter to six: Some of the fathers are sitting in the recreation room when a Simba enters and steals a hat. In the meantime we hear a little more on the subject of sanctions against the whites. They each received four punches, except one who received only three—because he was a brave type...

Evening falls and all is peaceful.

Friday, September 4

We passed a very ugly night. About quarter after midnight (I was not yet asleep), a car drove up close to our rooms, just up to the garage. We heard some soldiers get out and scream, "Father, hey Father, wake up!" They enter onto the porch, bang their guns up against the windows, and I hear Father Kuypers talking to them. They want to see Father Frans Waldram, the "father of the batteries." He was still sleeping despite all the racket. When I went out, they were just saying what a good father he was. Almost all of them were drunk; they had found a truck full of beer. They then left. We don't know why they came. I got up, we smoked a cigarette together, and we went back to bed. During breakfast, we found out that most people had not heard a thing. All the better.

At eleven thirty: It was a peaceful morning. One car came, only to recharge a battery. Last night I learned why they're running down their batteries so fast. They stop the motor and then leave the lights on.

At five o'clock: A calm afternoon. Just before tea time Father Kraewinkels had to sell his radio for five hundred francs. At the mission it is less peaceful than here: they are coming and going constantly with all sorts of screaming and threats.

At five past eight: Some of these characters came back to pretend that they were as poor as Job. They also wanted to "take part" in recreation, but when the others entered, they preferred to take their leave. I think we have an advantage here: an important group stops them from being so brutal. Around six o'clock, there were a few gunshots. Calm evening, if you discount the constant passage of vehicles.

Saturday, September 5

At eleven o'clock: We've just come back, in silence and completely exhausted. At seven thirty, we were obliged to go down to the Territory. It was awful. The fathers were the first. There were a lot of people there already. They were demanding that the brothers arrive. We were all assembled there before the dock for the ferryboat. They demanded that the sisters come down. A truck full of soldiers went in search of them. In the meantime they permitted us to look for some shade. After about forty-five minutes or an hour (you lose track of time, you know!), we had to all go up in front of the office of the Territory, near the flagpole, where the executions had taken place before. In the meantime, the sisters arrive. There are a few white sisters who aren't there. All the black sisters are there. The flag is raised in the midst of a deadly silence. Eight prisoners that they've been roughing up for an hour and making dance sit in a row on the ground. Among them is the father of one of the black sisters, one of the better Catholics of Bondo. Their names are read from a list, they are presented as members of the political party RADECO, and the people are asked to confirm this by "acclamation." The execution then begins. The first passes into a hedge of soldiers. He is pierced by several bayonets and then decapitated.

One cannot explain the sadism of these acts. The second is killed by blows with several clubs. The third is shot. A fourth is killed by a "little brat" with shots from a pistol; then some "adult soldiers" finish him off. When it came time for the father of our black sister (we were trying to hide her in back of us so that she wouldn't see anything), she had to advance in front to see all. Hideous! The three prisoners left were put on the side and so, for the time being, are spared. For the grand finale, the soldiers began to fire into the air. During this whole ordeal, there were soldiers stationed here and there among us in order to suppress any reaction. After that, we had a speech from the "big chief" via microphone. At the end, all the whites had to pass before the big chief in order to render him homage and to give witness of our submission to the new regime. After that we were able to go home. Those executed, even if we don't call them "martyrs," were very heroic. We learn afterward that they were praying all week long in their prison cells. It seems that the father of the black sister was their "chief." He was one of the most active Christians in Bondo.

At three o'clock: The mood here isn't very great. During the meal, they came to get the motorcycle of Father van Heeswijk. We don't care anymore. Let them come. They will take everything anyway.

At quarter past five: Everybody is going to the football field. There is a big celebration of dancing there to top off the "liberation." We can already hear the deafening sound of the drums. If they keep this up all night we will not get any sleep.

At quarter past eight: Around quarter to eight, I wanted to go to the recreation room, when a group asked me to accompany them to the "evening dance." The diocesan priest Father Jean thought that we ought to show up. They were not very threatening. I accompanied them. We were six, three blacks (Brother Pierre, Father Jean, and Brother Henry) and three whites (Fathers Vissers and Jansen and myself). Along the way Father Jean told us that they (the "chiefs") had invited us and that we ought to go and that we would be welcome. A group of the Youth who followed us was singing a song about the "dirty Flemish," but at a signal from Father Jean, they shut up. I was not comfortable. The football field resembled a dancing swamp. Each tribe had its corner and was doing its own traditional dances.

Fr. Albert Timmers, osc
(35 years old)

Fr. Marinus Godefrooy, osc
(52 years old)

Fr. Jan van Oort, osc
(38 years old)

They noticed us and I felt fairly at ease. We made a round of the field, shaking hands as we went along, and then we returned home after about a half-hour.

Halfway home we met the two brats with the motorcycle of Father van Heeswijk: it was already ruined.

Around seven o'clock: The people are coming back already from "the ball." They want to get home before nightfall.

Up to now, this was the most difficult day for us.

Sunday, September 6

At eleven thirty: Despite a fairly peaceful night, most of us didn't sleep well. It's understandable. When we were on our way to the High Mass this morning, some soldiers came to ask for a watch. It was very tense as we refused, and they finally responded by saying: "The priests of Bondo are bad men, only wait a while and we will get even." Just when Mass was starting, the brothers who work in the garage were called to repair a car that had caught fire. They finished the job about eleven o'clock.

After dinner: During the meal, it is said that the whites will again be called to the Territory on the subject of the prices for things. Another rumor is going around: Some Simba will be in prison. Where is the truth?

At three thirty: After a calm morning, Brother Leonard brings us some good news. The diocesan priest Father Jean (to whom we owe a lot) was this morning at the Territory asking for a furlough to go and get his sister at Lobi. The captain had a lot of work to do: all the Simba had to present themselves to him. Moreover, several of them were already in prison. They had to hand over all that they had stolen. The captain began with the lieutenant, who, among others, had directed the looting of Lobi. Father Jean declared again all that had been stolen. The captain was very friendly and hung on the cassock of Father Jean a medal of Lumumba. Now we understand the communiqué that was sent to us this morning, according to which no one could come into the mission under pain of punishment. As long as this captain is here, we will pass some peaceful days.

At ten minutes to seven: Everything is peaceful. The sisters of Titule have come for a visit. We can walk around again. We are discussing the school problem. Radio Stanleyville had said something about classes starting up again. But there are so many problems. We have not been able to begin the religion classes for converts. There is even less hope to begin classes for the girls. And who will occupy himself with the boys, where to find them? Brother Leo comes to tell us that Jan Janssen has won the world championship of road bicycling. Indeed, life continues elsewhere; sometimes we forget it.

At nine o'clock: By chance we hear a speech by President Gbenye on the radio. He says that he is against neither religion nor the missionaries.

Monday, September 7

Peaceful morning. Some cars come for batteries; that's it.

At quarter to eleven: I come back from having made a tour of the garage. There's a lot going on down there! Five or six soldiers and some members of the Youth are loitering around there while the brothers and some fathers are at the disposal of these "gentlemen" for repairing whatever. Since yesterday, the soldiers are considerably calmer. I hear that some sisters came to speak to Father Kuypers. We have again a little more liberty to move around.

At quarter past three: The peace is holding. A student from the high school has come to see me. He reports that one has become more severe with the Simba. They can no longer beat up the people and are being punished. The lieutenant was punished in public. This young man wanted to do some shopping in the stores while there still is something…but there was a big crowd there and the Simba were letting their families and friends get first in the lines. So he wasn't able to buy anything.

At five o'clock: I've just learned, at the coffee break, that the Popular Republic of the Congo has proclaimed itself. The new government is at Stanleyville. Another thing that we've learned, if I understand correctly, is that we are living under a communist regime here.

A peaceful evening.

Tuesday, September 8, the Birth of Mary

After dinner: Everything is calm. Last night a car arrived around three o'clock: they brought back a lifting-jack. Almost everybody was awakened. There is still no news on the subject of the opening of the school year. It's said that the captain will stay here yet about ten days or so, in order to get everything organized; after…we will see!

At five o'clock: A calm day. Only Father Frans Waldram is called to work for recharging batteries. There are all sorts of vehicles, even from Stanleyville. He really has too much work to do. A motor was running all day long. There's talk again of a plane that's been flying over Bondo.

At seven o'clock: The diocesan priest Father Jean has obtained his papers authorizing him to use the sisters' car from Baye for whatever is useful. By Radio Hilversum we learn that about fifteen women will participate in the third session of the (Second Vatican) Council. Here, we had forgotten that the Council is going on. The evening: some beer.

Wednesday, September 9

Papa's birthday. For a good month now, all correspondence between me and the family has been blocked. Undoubtedly, they are worried. The night and the morning: peaceful.

At ten o'clock: Suddenly, all the workers have to go to the Territory. They go. They come back a little later and say that they can no longer work today because, they say, a lot of soldiers have fallen at Yakoma.

At twelve thirty: We receive the news from Yakoma. It seems the soldiers are in a battle at Yakoma; seven have been killed, and there are four wounded here at the hospital.

At five thirty: Sister Paula arrives with a defective radio. She has news of the wounded. One is wounded in the back (by a bullet), another was hit in the pelvis, and another between his shoulders. Yesterday, a thief was also killed. They made him kneel down along the shore of the Uele, shot his back full of holes, and then pushed him in the water. The reason why the soldiers have been wounded, they say, is because they have had relations with women, which is forbidden. It reduces to nothing their immunization against bullets. Today, a whole group departed for Yakoma, with the intention of killing everybody. As for the whites here present, the situation is miserable. Some of them are ill. One is in danger of death and would like to go to Bangassou.

Around seven o'clock, a new whim on the part of the Youth of Mulo: They want a battery.

THURSDAY, SEPTEMBER 10

On coming back from the brothers', I spot at least thirty soldiers near the garage. They had been to the "war" in Yakoma. They are very mild-mannered. Some of them ask for some books of prayer from the pastor. Yesterday evening, Radio Stanleyville announced that there will be something today at Bondo with the committee.

At four o'clock: A peaceful day. After a restful siesta (interrupted only by some soldiers who came to claim a battery that some others had already come for this morning), I went to the garage. A truck loaded with soldiers (I should say "little soldiers") arrived at precisely that moment. They were going to the war. They had perhaps three rifles for the entire group. The others had material of a more traditional type: spears, knives, and clubs of wood or of iron.

At quarter past eight: Slowly there is news filtering in from the "front." One of those killed was a former carpenter of Brother Leonard's. The soldier who came to get the motor scooters of Fathers van Heeswijk and Snijkers was also killed. He wasn't yet 20 years old; he was the former chief scout at Buta.

Another story: A soldier arrived at the brothers' demanding a motorcycle. He left with the cycle. The other soldiers went after him. They found him at Likati, and they killed him immediately. In the meantime, all the cars of the mission have departed, even the one that no one was to touch. They had need of it to transport the wounded.

It is now estimated that about five hundred soldiers have left for Yakoma. The soldiers who came these last few days for batteries (and they were numerous!) were all very friendly. At the garage, too, their attitude was more human.

FRIDAY, SEPTEMBER 11

During this past week, our situation has noticeably improved as far as several things go. They don't come and steal or loot in such a silly way as before. We can again play our tape recorders, and we can take our radios out of hiding. We are definitely breathing better. We aren't as afraid as before. Yet there remains a certain doubt: we and the Premonstratensians have not done anything for a whole month. What's going to happen? All our communications with Europe have been interrupted. We don't know anything about other dioceses. Besides this incertitude, you notice a certain discouragement in yourself and also in others: why are we here? The gulf between us and the people gets deeper and deeper. No one has any confidence anymore in anyone. Are we, as white people, solely by our presence a psychological block for the black people in finding a solution to their problems? For some three years, there has developed in the people a certain envy (or jealously) towards us. Their misery gets worse, whereas our riches are the same (people don't believe what they see). These people would themselves have probably taken part in the looting, if the soldiers had not been so severe toward those who steal. When one thinks like this at certain moments, you get depressed. Some think that the situation now is very different from the situation of 1960: the people are not against us at the moment. Surely, they have to be with us, but one doesn't know how to discern their feelings. One could believe the contrary.

At ten past ten: I just came from taking a peek at the garage. A car loaded with the wounded was leaving for Stanleyville. In the front was someone seriously wounded: the carpenter of Brother Leonard, who is therefore not dead. In the back were three who appeared to be less gravely hit.

At twenty past three: Father Frans Waldram comes to tell us that the news we heard that the lieutenant had been tied up and taken to Stanleyville was entirely true.

At quarter past eight: We hardly hear a thing on the subject of Yakoma. Someone had reported (and this is the last news that we've had) that the war was approaching its end, that the rebels would be victorious and would indeed have killed all the men at Yakoma. That seems exaggerated.

Saturday, September 12

I just came back from the garage. The Simba who had stolen the motorcycle of Father Carremans of Lobi had to bring it back.

The engine is now at the garage, complete with a notice from the commander, according to which the engine is from Lobi and ought to be brought back there. The sisters' pickup truck was also brought back. For how long? One hears now that a white man and his wife were killed at Yakoma. That should be the Dutchman Cornelissen, but we can't put much credence in this news. Even so, this gives you some fear.

At one o'clock: The communiqués coming from Yakoma are a little more "comforting." No one was assassinated. Only some soldiers have fallen. In the meantime, a major has arrived here. Brother Marcel tells us that all the defective cars suffer from the same problem: cranks melted down. What's left of the day passes peacefully.

Sunday, September 13

Yesterday evening we experienced a terrific storm. Lightning struck a palm tree close to the dwelling of Monsignor Creemers. The tree began to burn up, but the rain quickly put it out. The ground around the tree was literally all turned up. All the lights went out. But the damages don't seem to be too bad.

I just got back from the High Mass. During the service, a soldier came into the church, made the sign of the cross, and then went in search of some young men to push a car. After the Mass, Brother Joost Sleeckx of the Premonstratensians asked if he could help out at the garage: Brother Marcel had not yet found the time to go to Mass.

The administrator showed up at one of the white's and presented him with a list of fees for some officials and asked him to pay them. It's in this disgusting way that they discourage people from staying in this country.

At eleven o'clock: Fifteen minutes ago, some soldiers paid us the honor of a visit. I just barely had the time to shut off my radio. They came to have their watches fixed. They were very friendly. One of them spoke in almost current French. He's probably a student. I would like to know how many of our boys are still free. It's silly, but almost all the youth are given the name "Simba."

Someone recounted to the fathers from Buta that one of the diocesan priests from down there had been killed. It was Father Etienne. It could be true because he was known as a sympathizer of

Fr. Hendrik Verberk, osc
(48 years old)

Fr. Rob Carremans, osc
(55 years old)

Fr. Gerard Kester, osc
(47 years old)

RADECO. About two o'clock this afternoon, someone will come here and all of us will have to present ourselves with a list of all our names.

At five o'clock: No one has come so far. The list is ready. A few minutes later, somebody came to get the list, and we did not have to all present ourselves. So much the better.

This evening, we have received for the first time in a month a visit from the Brothers of Saint Gabriel. We learn that the bicycle thief has been killed. One guesses that there have been already about twenty-five deaths in Bondo.

At five minutes to nine: Three of us were occupied listening to the radio this evening, when we suddenly heard a cracking noise very dry and near. We hid the radio and went out. The usual spectacle: doors opening up and men asking what's going on. We don't hear or see anything more. This incident is typical of the kind of atmosphere that reigns here. The rest of the evening passed in peace.

Monday, September 14, Exaltation of the Cross

At ten thirty: The feast of the Order had begun particularly well. At ten o'clock (I was in my room), I heard the cries of some soldiers, which I hadn't heard for some time. A soldier suddenly entered my room: "Outside. Join the other fathers. Get going fast!" Father Kuypers comes out of his room at the same time. The other fathers are assembled before the dining room. We have to take off our socks and shoes. They are thrown into a pile. Then we had to go, in naked feet, to look for our papers. All the house boys also had to come. The cook received a blow from a rifle butt and had to go get a bed sheet that would serve to gather up our socks and shoes. In the meantime, they go nosing around in all our rooms, crying out that we have hidden some Americans! They stop the inspection of our rooms. Another soldier arrives who says that we can put our socks and shoes back on. Then we have to go, one following the other like geese, to the mission. One soldier tries to mock us as we get into line, but a former student of our schools stops him. Some mock us, and others speak to us in a friendly manner. One doesn't know any longer on which foot to dance. We have to put ourselves in a row, and our papers are checked and compared with the list that we had to turn in yesterday. Then we have to turn in all our keys. They say that they are going to use them for a "thorough" inspection. We say to them: "There are dozens of rooms and hallways at the seminary, and you will never sort out all the keys!" They think the same way, and so we all go together with them to show them our own rooms. Once we arrive at our destination, the inspection begins, for the fourth time? They find a tape deck in the room of Father Theo Hacken. The apparatus and the tapes have to be taken by the boys to the commander who's at the mission. There's discussion of a ham radio that we should have. It has to come out, and then later, they want to talk about a disc for receiving and sending signals. In the other rooms they seize anything that isn't nailed down. Anything that appears complicated and that has some wires is studied and examined... In my room, they find the first radio. I tell them that it's a gift from my mother and I show them her photo. That's okay. Another finds the chalice of Father Huub van Lieshout. The chief enters and says, "Leave that, it belongs to God." They want to take my razor, until one of the Simba explains that it has nothing to do with a receiver because it's used to shave with...And so this goes on until they come to the room of Father Kraewinkels, and suddenly one of the military police arrives. He shows them his armband and asks them if they know what that means. He begins to scold the chief because of their nosing around in everything and carrying everything off. They are not in agreement; they go aside and continue their discussion in a low voice. The M.P. comes back and tells us that we can go back to our rooms in peace. The others look around a bit more, but they soon all depart. Father Frans Waldram lost his watch; however, they brought back the tape deck of Father Hacken.

Everything is again peaceful.

At quarter past five: Some things are beginning to become clearer. The rumor is going around among the soldiers that sixteen Americans are roving around in the vicinity, dressed in cassocks. They have with them an apparatus for broadcasting. Surely, this would scare them.

N. B. I am taking up again the diary in Stanleyville, on September 21. I will try to describe how we have come from Bondo to Stanleyville, day by day, insofar as I can remember it.

The Evening of the Exaltation of the Cross: About eight thirty, a truck arrives at the seminary with eight soldiers. All of us have to accompany them immediately. Then we go to the brothers'. Some soldiers enter: they steal some radios and all the money, and old Brother van Loon is beaten, while the others stand by in their bare feet. It goes on and on. Everything is turned over and inside out. In the meantime, we have to wait in the truck. That goes on until eleven o'clock. All the white brothers join us in the truck, and we return to the seminary. There they ask who the "patron" of the seminary is. Father van Heeswijk identifies himself. They want to know how much money he has. He cites a figure, and several men accompany him. They take all the money and a pile of other stuff. On coming back, they pass the rooms of Fathers Snijkers and Kraewinkels. Here they turn over all the drawers and armoires, they steal a tape deck, and piles of other things are thrown on the floor and they take some of it. Our dog begins to react, but after a blow on the snout with a rifle butt, one doesn't hear any more of him. Then the truck rolls over to the prison. They lock us up, about twenty people, in a cell about 6.5 feet by 10 feet. One of the Brothers of Saint Gabriel begins to vomit. It's hot and it stinks. In a corner there is a large bucket, which is our bathroom. It fills its role, humiliating as it can be, until morning. We're there all night. We can't all sit down, so we establish a schedule for sitting or standing, and we try to get some sleep. During the night, we hear some women crying in a cell next to ours: are they the sisters? We don't know anything about the fathers at the mission. Are they also imprisoned? Or are they still down there? Tonight, in this hole in the wall, is our most awful night. Some of us are upset and sick. There is a tendency to faint. And this goes on until eight o'clock in the morning.

Tuesday, September 15

In the morning they have us come out of our hole and they take us to a bigger room, where we find the fathers and brothers of the mission, who have been there since two o'clock in the morning. It appears that the sisters are also imprisoned. A little later, they let out the brothers who work in the garage, Father Frans Waldram (for the batteries), and those who work in the kitchen. We breathe a little easier. When they come back, they are carrying some necessary things: some blankets, identity papers, soap, razors, etc. …The diocesan priest Father Jean comes to visit us, and he is moved. Nevertheless, he speaks to us about being courageous. When will we be freed? Why are we prisoners? Why was all that money stolen, for everything was taken away from the mission? Besides all this, they stole about a million Belgian francs. They are talking about an order to arrest all the missionaries. They will be brought to Stanleyville. All of a sudden, we hear a cry in the room where the sisters are imprisoned: one of them stepped through the planks and tore open an artery in her leg. She was bleeding a lot and was immediately taken to the convent.

About four o'clock in the afternoon, the fathers and the brothers of Baye arrive. There is a lot of commotion: we are wondering what's become of Monga and Lobi? Will they come also? There's a lot of talking, and we come to understand that similar things happened at Baye as had happened at Bondo. All day long, some chiefs of the Simba come to do some inspections and to speak. There is no agreement in their hierarchy. Some of them want to drive us to Stanleyville (by way of Buta) and others think that it's ridiculous, because everything is going well here and they want to send a telegram and wait for an answer.

In the evening the mechanics from the garage come back and we get settled for the night. We sleep on some newspapers or, for example, three on one blanket. Close to morning, it gets terribly cold. There's a breeze that passes under the door. Some are able to sleep a little.

During the night, it suffices to knock at the door to be able to go and use the toilets. This becomes important, since one of us is suffering from diarrhea. In the middle of the night they come to look for Father (Marinus) Godefrooy. He has to accompany them to Baye where they will look for the fathers who stayed there. These arrive in the morning. Happily they were able to bring along some useful items.

Wednesday, September 16

The sisters who were not imprisoned come to bring us

something to eat along with some bedding. We are now able to walk a bit outside. Today the sisters imprisoned with us are able to return home. We think that we also may be able to return home and so we pack up our things; however, nothing happens.

We are going to spend another night in prison. Each of us now has a blanket and that's already quite a bit. We feel ourselves to be very "detached." Most of us have a plank on which to sleep; others sleep right on the ground. Those who work at the garage are able to sleep there.

Thursday, September 17

We receive a new "keeper" of the prison. He looks for ways to give trouble to those who bring us food. We hope again that we will be able to go home today. In the meantime Brother Leonard feels really sick. Sister Paula comes to see him. They bring along a mattress, and afterward he receives a shot, so now he feels a bit better. During the day, some soldiers come to see us. Some are very friendly and the others take us for imbeciles. We're getting used to it.

In the evening, we learn that we will again pass the night in prison. Will those who work at the garage be able to sleep there? We receive a response to this question about eleven o'clock: everyone is brought to the prison, Father Frans Waldram also. Now we are all here divided into two rooms.

Some new blankets are brought to us by the black sisters and brothers. Each one is thinking of us.

Friday, September 18

Upon awaking, there is a tense atmosphere. The Simba don't come to get the mechanics for the garage and we wonder why.

It begins to rain "cats and dogs." Water threatens to enter under the door of the place where we are. Hours and hours pass. In all this rain, the sisters arrive bringing us food and a whole stack of things: cushions, underwear, other clothes, and some more blankets. For the first time, we are fairly well set up. For example, each one has his own cushion, and that will bring us a lot of comfort in the days and nights to come. They also brought some medicines, which brings up another point: everybody is suffering from something—one has no appetite,

Fr. Arnold Vervoort, osc
(40 years old)

Fr. Willem van Wetten, osc
(46 years old)

These two were killed at Dakwa, along with an English sister and a Portuguese merchant (also see the February 10 entry).

another can't sleep, a third is constipated.

Around noon, the rain lets up a bit.

Around two o'clock, the door suddenly opens. The order is given: Everybody immediately into the truck along with all his affairs; they're waiting to get going. Are we going home? We start out and turn on the road going in the opposite direction towards the Uele River. That strengthens our belief that we're leaving for Buta and then on to Stanleyville. This is something that we've been talking about for days.

Under the stares of those who are not very friendly, we set out on the ferryboat and pass to the other side of the river. The expedition continues on the bad road to Buta. The ambiance is very restless. Near Likati, where we arrive about five o'clock, there is a roadblock where we are very badly received. They treat us like real prisoners who have done something wrong. They threaten us with lances but do not touch anyone. They cry everywhere "Mateka," which means in Lingala "butter" but in Kiswahili seems to mean something like "booty of war." They also say, "Give us one of these guys so that we can rough him up."

Our first important stop is at Likati. We stop near the building of the C.V.C. Upon arriving in Likati we passed by a jeep, and now the soldiers are in a discussion. They have no confidence in these guys. They follow them, they telephone, etc. Finally, the jeep comes back. Their papers seem to be an order. They threaten us again, but the soldiers who are accompanying us protect us. These are some brave boys. Finally, we can get down and stretch our legs. After a stop of two and one-half hours at least, we are back on the road. We arrive at Dulia around nine thirty. We learn later that some other fathers came this way and were beat up. As far as we go, the soldiers' behavior has been correct.

After some cries of "Mateka," they become friendly and give us some benches and some bananas, while a wood fire agreeably warms us up. The Youth are going to prepare supper for our escorts, and that evidently takes a long time. About eleven thirty, we start out again. Most of us are very tired. Around two or two thirty, we stop again about three miles from Buta. The folks there give us something to drink. We talk a bit, and then we begin the last leg of the journey. The soldiers say that they have to bring us to the military camp. How are they going to react there? I don't know if we care or if we don't care a hoot. Around three o'clock, we stop before the prison. We hope that they will let us sleep at the mission or at the hospital, but nothing of that. We can sit or lie down on the large porch or in the halls of the prison. We don't hear anything more about food. There are prisoners in the cells, some Simba, and they call the guards and ask who we are. During the whole night, they talk, they scream, and they laugh. Some of them never shut an eye. For myself, I sat down on the floor and I fell asleep. We stayed there, along with our stuff, three hours, like the bums of Paris ("les clochards de Paris").

Saturday, September 19

They wake us up at six o'clock for check-in. We are not anything great to behold. Around us the usual life of prison goes on, in the same way that we knew it in Bondo: they beat the prisoners, there's a line up for those who go to the toilets, another to wait behind, etc. They tell us: "We are going to take you to the mission." We wait; nothing happens. It goes on and on. The curious come to look at us. First it's eight o'clock, then nine, and finally ten. We have to line up on the big porch in front of the prison and then to sit down. It's just like kindergarten. They give us the usual speech. We can stand up. About eleven thirty, a truck arrives and transports us to the mission. Bishop Jacques Mbali is waiting for us, surrounded by the sisters and the black Marist brothers. We finally feel good: we can finally relax, sit down in a chair, and, after a whole week, be more or less free in our way of acting. We receive a hot meal. What a luxury...They say that they will come to get us at two o'clock. After the meal, we again wait...until four thirty. In the meantime, Bishop Jacques tells us how he had been condemned to death and that the people revolted and saved him. He had passed some bad times, and you could tell. At the mission, we get some clean underwear, new sandals, and all sorts of things. Just as we had received the Premonstratensians at our place, so now they do the same for us.

The truck comes and we get on. The bishop gives us his blessing and we set off. We have some new drivers, and they are friendlier than the ones we had from Bondo to Buta. The ambiance is good.

One of the drivers says, "Keep talking. If you don't, you'll worry too much and that's not good for you." It's the same for them; they talk endlessly. Thanks to them, the mood gets better and better. We had just departed, and the motor gives out. So, back to the mission house we go. The mechanics get to work, and a half-hour later we depart. We have in the meantime placed a canvas over the back of the truck because there's a storm that's threatening. On the way, we have to stop regularly because several of us suffer from diarrhea. That's due to eating cold meat during the trip. The driver stays cool, and he stops each time. We get as far as Banalia, where there is a large river to cross. On arriving at the ferryboat we hear and see some dancing. We stop. Some priests come out of the night. It's the group from Bumba. They are in the "same boat" as we are. They also must go to Stanleyville. They have good companions, but they are spending the whole night in the village. There is a feast and the Simba are invited. They talk about all they have been through and that they are still alive, and they will tell us more at Stanleyville. We continue on until arriving at the ferryboat. In the meantime it's one thirty in the morning. The crossing is long. It's cold and we feel really miserable. Finally we arrive at the other shore. Will we pass the night in prison? No, happily we roll on toward the mission. The fathers offer us a cup of coffee, and we set ourselves up in the dining room for the night. Three members of the Youth pass the night with us, lance in hand to guard us, but they don't bother us.

Sunday, September 20

We get up at six o'clock. We are authorized to attend Mass: today is Sunday. Our group of dirty fathers and brothers, still half asleep, is noticed as we walk into church. After Mass we eat some bread with butter and jam and drink some coffee. This finally wakes us up. The fathers we met at the river were supposed to arrive two hours ago and finally show up. We learn that they also were pillaged and shaken up quite a bit. It's probably the same all over.

The truck arrives at ten thirty, and we leave. We first pass by the Territory building. We get off here, and we sit on the chairs that had been prepared. Here, we have to make a list of all present. The list from Bondo doesn't look good because some of us, being sick, had stayed at Buta. This was thanks to the intervention of a Dutch doctor, Doctor Vinken of Roermond. And so it was that Brothers Peerke and Leonard and Father Polydoor Carremans stayed at Buta. At Banalia, they let a Premonstratensian go, one that they know well. From the large porch of the Territory building, we have a view of the river. There's a crowd down there. Without a doubt some big shot is going to show up. When he arrives, they shoot in the air, sing, and dance. And then the soldiers "parade." They pass by us, and their looks are not very friendly. If they let a troop so excited get at us, we would be cut up into pieces. At noon, we finally leave for Stanleyville. We encounter the same threats on the road, but our drivers are good. Afterward, we learn that the group of fathers from Aketi was not so lucky. Their truck hit another. They stopped. The other truck was full of soldiers who mounted the fathers' truck, and there were plenty of blows.

It's about thirty-two miles to Stanleyville, and we notice again that Africa is certainly the country of a thousand surprises. We ask our soldiers if they don't have a little water for us. "No," they say, "in a little while at Bengamisa, you will have some beer." We stop, and they bring us some cases of beer. They pass us the bottles. It all goes around quickly, and soon each of us has a bottle up to his mouth. We drink a lot, but finally we must refuse. The soldiers want to give us more bottles. We accept some, because African good manners demand it: you can never refuse anything. The mood is better. We are able to get off the truck. They bring more beer. People are coming from all over. Little groups form. And you notice that the fathers and the brothers are mixed in with the population. It is impossible to drink all this beer. We're there about a half-hour when this luxurious automobile arrives. It's Gbenye in person, the president of the new "regime" who is driving. He does not look happy. A soldier tries to hide his bottle behind his back. The "president" does not seem to understand why these fathers and brothers are coming to Stanleyville…something we do not understand either.

We quickly get back on the truck. The soldiers say that we cannot arrive in Stanleyville with our dirty clothes. They stop before Stanleyville. They say that we must go immediately to see the colonel. When we get to the "highway," they stop. But we all do not have another cassock to change into. Finally, it's settled. We are to go to the business office of the mission. There we are received with open arms by a big crowd. We are the last group. Those of Aketi, Bumba, and Lolo arrived before. We are lodged in the print shop, and there are enough foam rubber mattresses. We have to quickly wash and change because we are to have a meeting with Gbenye yet this evening, say the soldiers. But nothing happens. All the better.

After a good supper, during recreation, the other groups tell us about their adventures. On the whole, our group was the better treated. Almost all the others were beaten up. They crazily assaulted Bishop Waterschoot of Lolo. Several fathers and brothers wear bandages on the head or eyes. Some were even beat up here in Stanleyville at the military camp. During the night, we sleep like rocks.

Monday, September 21

It is a peaceful day but with disturbing communications and news. We hear the story of the first week in Stanleyville, during which hundreds, and probably thousands, of people were murdered. The Dutch consul arrives, followed by the Belgian consul. In the meantime, a delegation goes to see Gbenye. He is very friendly and says that everything that has happened concerning our trip down here has been due to a misunderstanding. He promises to give back all the stolen money and to send soldiers to reestablish order. He would like us to be able to return as soon as possible.

Tuesday, September 22

Another peaceful day. Stanleyville seems to be a solid city. We would like to stay here a while, but the communications concerning our departure become more numerous. We wait. In the meantime, the whites of Stanleyville bring or send all sorts of packages; there are still about a thousand whites here. They bring everything: toothbrushes, shirts, pants, cigarettes, etc.

Wednesday, September 23

Several of us have to go see Gbenye again this morning. Everybody is obliged to go back to their post. Those who refuse can leave the country by way of the Sudan. The morale descends again.

A little before eleven o'clock, we eat, for they tell us that we are going to depart immediately.

Around noon, a bus of the C.V.C. arrives. After a lot of discussion, the groups from Lolo and Bumba will be the first to go. We say our "good-byes" with best wishes. That doesn't mean anything to them: the battles are terrible in the region of Bumba. Even so, they leave with a lot of courage.

After that, they tell us that there are no other means of transportation. Again, wait. Some lie down and go to sleep. Our "baggage" is ready. A second bus arrives around two o'clock. Those in the bus, from someplace or other, come out, though they don't seem happy about it. The colonel can be regularly seen milling about in all this going and coming. At first view, he gives the agreeable impression of a fat little man. We eat another sandwich. Then, the consul of Holland arrives with some letters from the Red Cross. In this way, we are also able to send a few words home. We have hopes that the letters will arrive at their destination. So, our families will know that it isn't so bad for us down here.

The bus waits. Only those of Bondo can get on. We can get settled fairly comfortably. It's a real bus. We have to wait yet for the money that they are going to give us. We go over to the residence of the colonel. We get off the bus; they bring us chairs and all the Simba are very friendly; we are no longer prisoners. We have nothing with which to reproach ourselves. We wait. It's now quarter to five. The colonel comes out. The question of the money will be regulated, he says, and he also says that it's now too late for us to depart, so we will depart tomorrow morning. We return to the diocesan business center. We are entitled to another peaceful night. In the evening, we have some whiskey.

Thursday, September 24

We're supposed to depart about six or six thirty. But we have enough experience with these schedules now! It's nine o'clock when we do depart. The trip to Banalia is pleasant. We notice that everybody must know of the desires of Gbenye that we be treated well. Everywhere, we are received as friends. Everybody acclaims us and is happy. During the trip we discuss some of the reasons for the hectic things we've had to endure. Here are a few of our deductions: 1) there was a rumor going around among the soldiers that there were some Americans here disguised as "fathers"; 2) somewhere unknown the "fathers" were supposed to have set up a transmitter and that would really have excited some suspicions; 3) there are certainly some members of the sect of Kibangu among the Simba and their members have always been against the missionaries. They would have profited from the opportunity to do us some harm; and 4) there was a telephone message from Stanleyville saying that they should round up all the "mercenaries" and bring them to Stanleyville; they understood "missionaries" instead.

At Banalia we eat hastily. For a few days now, we aren't bothered by anyone.

On the way to Buta we meet up with some cars full of Simba, and their looks are not in the least friendly! This makes our morale sink again. The more we get further and further away from Stanleyville, we feel less secure. Then, all of a sudden, we see on the side of the road the bus that has the fathers from Lolo and Bumba. It's car trouble, something to do with the tires. Monsignor Waterschoot has already left in a very nice car with the major. Most of the others find a place in our bus, and we continue on. Around ten thirty, we arrive at Buta. We pass the prison and happily continue on toward the mission. Here, everything has been prepared for us. A fairly large group of Crosiers sleep in the girls' dormitory at the sisters. This is the first time in two weeks that we actually have a real bed.

The sisters have prepared a meal. We learn that the Capuchins of Yakoma and the Crosiers of Monga and Lobi are at Buta. They had spent the afternoon in prison but were liberated upon the arrival of the major. They are already asleep; they were exhausted. We will see them tomorrow. We go early to bed (a way of speaking…from habit).

Friday, September 25

In the morning, we see again our confreres from Monga and Lobi. They've lived through more than we have. They were beat up, and their houses were looted. They were put in prison both in Monga and at Buta.

The fathers of Yakoma were the principal victims. Among them is a Protestant doctor from their sector, Doctor Paul Carlson,[17] an American. They were all in prison in Bondo and had to cut the grass around the prison with a scythe for seven hours straight.

It's peaceful until ten thirty. Then the news falls: those from Bumba and Bondo must depart immediately.

At quarter past four: We are still at Buta. As usual the soup is not as hot when one eats it as when one serves it. In the meantime, the most fantastic news arrives. Monga has been taken. They have already passed Lobi, and Bondo would be also entirely liberated. The atmosphere is tense. How can we go back in such conditions?

We stay here the entire day. At night, only the mournful barking of the dogs disturbs us.

Saturday, September 26

During Mass, we hear a bus that stops right in front of the mission. Those from Bumba have to depart. Indeed, about ten o'clock, the fathers of Lolo and of Bumba leave.

At three o'clock: Moments of tension. They say that they are coming to get the American doctor to take him to Stanleyville. We have learned that they have assassinated the American missionaries. The doctor is afraid and writes out his last will and testament. The Simba arrive but turn around and immediately go back.

At ten thirty: We have a peaceful evening. One of their bosses came to say that they will come to get us next Tuesday. Another reprieve! And we're not sad about it at all.

Sunday, September 27

We notice two Simba at the High Mass. Two loudspeakers announce a big meeting for the afternoon. Some black brothers go to attend. They don't say anything against the fathers. That's already something.

---

17 This is Doctor Paul Carlson from Torrance, California, who was sent as a medical missionary by the Evangelical Covenant Church. He was known for his excellent work and very compassionate ways. His entire family had been with him but was able to escape, while he remained in captivity.

The rest of the day is peaceful. We play billiards with the Marist brothers. Our American is always at the mission. Will they forget him?

Monday, September 28

A calm night. About eleven o'clock, the fathers from Yakoma, Lobi, and Monga have to go to the camp. A little later, they come and get the rest of us. And all of this for nothing! Another misunderstanding. The soldiers are not mean. The fathers of Yakoma, Monga, and Lobi get back their briefcases and trunks. On the other hand, the money that was in one of the briefcases has disappeared. After dinner, they tell us that those of us who are from Bondo are going to depart. We have to prepare everything for that which is going to follow.

We actually leave at four thirty. Our driver rolls speedily along, way too fast indeed. The first fifty-six miles toward Dulia pass without incident, and we arrive quickly in Likati. It's already dark; rolled up in our blankets, we are always going fast. Just about six miles from Likati, a shock throws the truck all over the road; it threatens to turn over, but we suddenly stop at the side of the road in the spillway. What happened? Grand confusion reigns. I lost my glasses and I hardly see a thing. We begin a search, and after ten minutes somebody finds them. Thank God! It seems that we really had good luck. The clutch was no longer working. Happily, the vehicle slipped into the spillway. The truck stopped after laboriously plowing up the ground. We tried to push; impossible to move it. We started digging but got nowhere. The soldiers go in search of help. They dig around, we push some more, but the truck won't budge. We begin to feel like this is going to be a long night. Before morning they bring us some bread and we eat a little. Eleven o'clock, noon…Some nap along the side of the road. The soldiers are going to look for more help. Those who arrive have some good shovels. They are able to completely dig out the vehicle, which begins to budge a little. We finally are able to get it into the middle of the road. We notice that the gear shift is bent back. The wheels are out of alignment. We are able to fix that with a crow bar. The work advances in this fashion until four thirty in the afternoon when we are able to begin once again. In the meantime, we congratulate Father Vissers who, at midnight, passed into his fifty-fifth year.

We begin the thirty-seven miles remaining. Everything is fine. But the driver is falling asleep, so Brother Marcel has to replace him at the wheel. We approach Bondo. We reach the Uele at five thirty in the morning. The day is dawning. Despite a lot of discussion, the service at the ferry refuses to take us across. At six thirty, we are still waiting. Finally, we are able to pass over in canoes with two trips. The welcome of the Simba is fairly reserved. The medicine man, who had stolen from our place, is also there. He stares us down, and during our crossing (because he is also in one of the canoes), he gives us a sermon: we should have tried our luck at Stanleyville, and so on and so forth. The atmosphere in Bondo is totally different than at Buta and Stanleyville, which hardly pleases us. Once on the other side, we wait a fair amount of time for a truck to take us home. In the meantime, a Simba whom we know comes to tell us that there are difficulties at Bondo. Everybody is in dispute. Then, one of the sisters arrives on a bike. The people have been alerted to our arrival. She is happy to see us safe and sound again. She departs immediately to prepare us some coffee.

Another time we pass through our familiar Bondo. Many people give us a sincere welcome. They are visibly happy to see us again. Groups of children run screaming behind the truck. Many people come to shake our hands as we descend from the truck and even while we're eating. This makes us feel good. Our dog is running all over. The black sisters had had him at their place.

The sisters and the diocesan priests arrive, for in addition to Father Jean there is also Father Jerome who has come from Bili. He informs us that things haven't been any better down there. "They" even amused themselves by playing in public with a chasuble and a monstrance. Our brothers who are there, Jef Wouters and Linus van Dijk, are fine. They haven't been beaten up, but the diocesan priests were. The major seminarian, Jean-Pierre of Monga, is also there. Some Simba also come to see us and are very friendly.

After the meal, we try to sleep a bit.

At six o'clock, an evening Mass at the brothers'.

In the evening, at the mission, we celebrate the birthday of

Father Willem Vissers by drinking the last bottles of beer. A happy thing to note: our rooms are intact. There was nothing more stolen. Dead from fatigue, we go to bed early.

Tuesday, September 29

We learn that 120 children have already presented themselves here at the high school, at the seminary, and at the normal school. The Simba went in search of them with two trucks. However, their papers were not in order, and so they had to be driven back home.

There are trucks regularly leaving Bondo, full of Simba, for the front at Yakoma. The news that the soldiers of the National Congolese Army had made some advances seem fairly uncertain.

After dinner, another group of soldiers departs; their truck meets up with another just coming back, which is full of the wounded. That makes such an impression on them that they turn around and come back. But they are quickly turned around again and head for the front. It seems that the Simba themselves are not happy with the commander. Some of the wounded Simba come to see us at the mission. They say that it's a question of a fairly important troop, and they are critical of their hierarchy. The other fathers have not yet arrived.

Wednesday, September 30

Both here at the seminary and at the mission it is absolutely peaceful. No one bothers us. There is never any news about the fathers who should be arriving.

Thursday, October 1

During the night, we hear trucks rolling by. Yesterday, there was a radio communication that announced that the missions should be left in peace. For the moment, here at Bondo, these orders seem to be well followed.

At eleven o'clock: The commander arrives at the mission. It seems that no one was around to welcome him, and he is very angry.

Friday, October 2

Today, Father Willem Vissers and the diocesan priest Father Jean visited the wounded here at the hospital. They were welcomed by the majority, and one even asked if he could go to confession, but just at that moment one of their big shots entered and purely and simply sent Father Willem on his way. The reason: it seems that the fathers had blessed the rifles of their adversaries. The fathers who should arrive from Buta are still not here.

Saturday, October 3

At eleven o'clock: We've just come back from a meeting at the Territory. A delegation, with the mission of calming the population, has arrived. We were forced to endure four speeches. They were already in session when we came in, but nobody made any remark. It was reassuring as they got into the matter. The first speech was appreciated with pleasure: like all the people of Bondo, the fathers belong to the opposing party. That must stop! We should have nothing to do but to occupy ourselves with our Masses and our schools. The population should get to work and not be afraid any longer. Another speaker cordially thanked us for not fleeing as some of the Europeans and the fathers of Buta did. That was a good move on our part and we should be congratulated…The presentation finished with a parade of troops. Thus, seeing that confidence in us had been restored, we left to go back home.

At four o'clock: The news that two canoes full of Simba had been turned over with everybody drowned seems to be true. The commander, who had stolen all of our money, was here for a moment. He was talking to Father van Heeswijk. He wanted to know what we had told President Gbenye and what we had asked for, and he promised to return next Monday to put in order this matter of "the money."

I just heard a good one. This morning, a soldier had stolen one of the puppies of our dog Puk, which is at the sacristan's house; the commander had demanded it. The wife of the sacristan, boiling with anger, went as soon as possible to see the commander. He didn't know anything about this story. He authorized the woman to take a few Simba with her, to find the guy, and to beat him up. They found him, and the puppy has come back. The soldier-thief is in prison. Still no word of the fathers from Buta. Did something happen to them?

Sunday, October 4

Yesterday, they came again to get three cows from the sisters.

There is never any word of the fathers who should have been following us. One soldier told us that they were en route, but that they had a breakdown and so had to return. For the rest, it's peaceful.

Monday, October 5

Our confreres are still not here. Today it's a week that we left Buta. Yesterday, no one bothered the mechanics at the garage because it was Sunday.

This morning, there was a Mass of the Holy Spirit for the opening of the school year. The two primary schools are functioning. The brothers want to begin some classes of orientation.[18] In the meantime, the problem of food is beginning to make itself felt. At the brothers' house, there are no longer any potatoes (moreover, there aren't any anywhere), nor is there any rice. Father van Heeswijk was able to help a little. For how long? During dinner, a Land Rover making a lot of noise rolled into the mission. Some officers got out... and asked the time of day! That's all.

After coffee: This morning there was reported a whole pile of things that have been stolen, among them the projector from the minor seminary, the tape deck of Father Snijkers, the electric harmonium belonging to the brothers at Baye, and there's no end to it. They came finally to talk about the money: that which Gbenye had not returned a while back. For all that which seems to be missing yet (and that's quite a bit!), they will do their best; many things have disappeared without a trace: some watches and transistors! These are things easy to carry away.

Tuesday, October 6

This morning, some soldiers asked Brother Marcel if he would bless their weapons; this is done in the National Congolese Army... Marcel sent them to the pastor, but they haven't showed up yet.

About five o'clock, someone showed up asking us if we were interested in buying some cards for the political party. But since we are not allowed to busy ourselves with politics, it didn't take long to

18 Upon the completion of high school, these classes would prepare one for his future direction, whether toward higher studies or some manual skill.

get rid of the guy.

The confreres from Buta have still not arrived. Where are they then?

Wednesday, October 7

Yesterday evening, during recreation, we again had the visit of a Simba. We thought at first that he was drunk. But, according to his own testimony, he was smoking marijuana. He was half-numb. He recounted the most bizarre incidents of the war. The absolutely strangest was on the subject of their invulnerability: it was sufficient for them to shake a handkerchief while crying out "*Mama Maria.*" This mother Mary was an old woman who was marching, completely nude, in front of the soldiers and who would catch the bullets in her handkerchief…for their adversaries, there was something similar: there, it was a soldier who was marching at their head with his mouth wide open: he swallowed all the bullets. They say that today there will be five truckloads of soldiers arriving. With that number, they could also bother us…

At quarter past four: We have just learned, from a black man, that our Congolese vicar-general of the diocese, Monsignor Daniel, is dead at Lovanium in Leopoldville. Is it true?

A Simba tells us that our fathers are still waiting for transportation from Buta.

Some boys from the bush come to ask for scissors from Father Kraewinkels; they are obliged to be "baptized" soon and they have to shave their skulls. Up until now, they have left the school kids in peace.

Thursday, October 8

My birthday. No news from my family for several months now. Everything is peaceful. Today I had work again, for the first time! The brothers opened their classes of orientation, and I gave some courses of religion. The children are very peaceful and cooperative.

Today, the soldiers are off duty. The battle should begin again tomorrow. Communications concerning the defeat of the rebels arrive more frequently: Beni, Uvira, Lodja. In certain places, the fathers have been freed and evacuated immediately. Will that happen here also, if…but we don't think so! Tomorrow, a European will be able to go to Bangassou to look for a special medicine for a sick child. We want to give him some mail or at least pass on some news that the fathers there might be able to write to Europe for us.

At noon, we had an alert. A telegram arrived: there are others coming. The schoolchildren have been sent home. They say that the National Congolese Army would be at Muma, so about fifty-five miles from Bondo. The tension mounts.

Friday, October 9

This morning we relived an event that had occurred earlier at the mission. A new group of rebels, freshly arrived from Stanleyville, forced their way, fairly violently, into the mission. They asked for people's papers and began to threaten things: they took two fathers with them. Afterward, they wanted bread. They did not receive it, but took it themselves anyway, and Brother Willem took it back. They were very angry when they left.

At eleven o'clock: Finally, our confreres from Buta arrive. Fortunately, the fathers from Yakoma and the American doctor are not with them. They are badly received here at Bondo: they are hit and stones are thrown at them.

Their departure was very difficult. Five times they had hit the road, and each time, there was some sort of car trouble and they had to return. Once they were already about six miles from Buta, and they had to return on foot.

Finally, everybody is fine, and we are happy that they have arrived. An important and more pleasant group gives us more security.

Saturday, October 10

At seven thirty in the morning: Two cars have already come by. They say that we have to go down to a meeting that will begin at eight o'clock; a new commander will arrive from Buta.

At ten thirty: We've just come back. Everything went well. Everybody was there: the sisters, the brothers, and all of us except the mechanics in the garage.

We first assisted at the raising of the flag and the singing of the anthem by the soldiers, of which there were about three hundred. Then there was a public training of the army. They started by firing blanks. All of us had to lie flat on the ground, but were not to be afraid. They threw a few grenades and then a tear-gas bomb.

When everybody was then heated up a bit, especially the soldiers, there was a barrage of words, this time entirely in our favor. The population should not be afraid, and the Simba would pay for everything that they wanted. To steal was strictly forbidden. The businessmen were, according to the speaker, wonderful guys and would soon have a leave to go to Bangui to look for all sorts of things that we needed. This was accompanied by a deafening applause: all the stores are empty. The speaker even spoke of "our friends the Europeans"...After a couple of tirades against the Americans and the fathers of Yakoma, we were able to go home.

Sunday, October 11

A lot of people were at the High Mass, even some Simba and their commander from Buta. After the Mass, there were a few who came to bother us at the seminary, but they were finally content to have a glass of water when they saw that it was impossible to steal a watch. Others came to buy a rosary; tomorrow, they leave for combat. According to some communications, which one is unable to check, they will fight tomorrow in two places: Yakoma and Muma.

Around noon, the secretary of the committee comes to explain to us that we did not act very intelligently in announcing officially in church that Monsignor Daniel had died at Leopoldville. In the first place, the information was given on a radio station from Leopoldville that the rebels do not recognize, and secondly, such information could sow confusion among the people during a state of war. We're a bit disturbed, but he should recognize our side of it, too: that the population knew it already, and if we did nothing about it, we could've been accused of ignoring the death of a black monsignor.

In the afternoon, we hear a lot of firing in the air. Also explosions from a few grenades.

Monday, October 12

They are saying that several trucks full of Simba have departed from here for the front. Here, they are firing all day long. They certainly have enough new munitions.

At quarter to noon: Some favorable communications are making the rounds: there was no battle. They say that they want to negotiate at higher levels. Is this true?

Tuesday, October 13

We hear reports that Monga and Lobi were terribly ravaged and pillaged. Even the altar cloths of Lobi were seen to be made into bandages. Fear reigns anew among the population. All the canoes are found on this side of the river.

Brother Lambert has been authorized to make a trip to Baye and return, of course under escort by a Simba. He is going to see how things are at the house, with the cattle and all the rest.

The Brothers of Saint Gabriel have opened all the classes at the normal school except the sixth. I give ten courses of religion there. Father van Lieshout teaches English and Father van Heeswijk arithmetic.

In the meantime, the earth is always turning: three Russian cosmonauts have come back safe and sound, Holland beat America in a tournament of water polo, the Vatican Council seems to be in an impasse, and Tshombe[19] has been welcomed with a crazy enthusiasm by the population of Leopoldville.

At noon, a black brother went to the depot to assure himself of the arrival of some boxes: they were there but had been emptied of their contents.

Wednesday, October 14

Several soldiers have been very bothersome these last few days: they come to ask for motorbikes, for motorcycles, for food. We put an end to that this morning, but for how long? They were occupied in pushing a motorcycle out of the garage; they wanted to take it to Stanleyville to have it repaired there. A Simba, who was not in agreement, left to alert the commander who immediately arrived, accompanied by some soldiers who were armed from head to toe. These guys were stripped of their helmets and weapons and were led

19 The president of Congo for the moment.

to prison.

The administrator came to the mission to announce the arrival of Gbenye: Bondo is going to receive the visit of the chief of state of the new power...He will probably arrive tomorrow. We were amiably requested to reserve a warm welcome for him.

Today, Brother Lambert tried to get on the road to Baye twice. The first time, a tire blew out after about five miles, and the second time, the car had to come back because they needed it once for something else.

Again, it was very peaceful today. There was no firing of guns, and all day long we didn't see even one Simba.

Thursday, October 15

Gbenye should arrive today. Some whites and others were waiting from two o'clock to four thirty. About four o'clock, most of the fathers and the sisters were at the Territory. A telephone call gave us the news that he is not even yet at Aketi. We all go home. Bondo has the aspect of a day of celebration, everything is cleaned up. Today, we receive some news from Ango: at the beginning of the "war," eighteen people were slain, among them an important chief and a good male nurse.

Today, Holland won four Olympic medals. This is indeed quite something, this liaison of Tokyo-Holland-Africa: at four o'clock these teams are rowing, and this evening we will have a report.

Friday, October 16

It seems that some mail has arrived. Gbenye is not yet here. For the rest, all is calm. In the evening, Radio Brussels gives the news from here: they speak of Yakoma and also of Bondo. It seems that the National Congolese Army has taken Bumba.

Saturday, October 17

Another Saturday: since the arrival of the rebels, there hasn't been one Saturday without something special happening.

This Saturday will not disappoint us either: during Mass, a car arrives and they inform us that Gbenye has arrived. Because of this, we have to eat rapidly so that we arrive on time for the big meeting, which will begin at seven thirty. In the half-hour that follows, several seemingly contradictory communications arrive. First of all, one says that some of the fathers can stay at home, for Gbenye is coming here yet on a visit. And then, they say that even so, all of us must come to the meeting. While on the way down there, we learn that Gbenye had wanted a solemn Mass with a *Te Deum*, but that couldn't take place, because he was in a hurry and wanted to get going as soon as possible to Ango. So we all went down to the Territory where we arrived at exactly seven thirty. The people were there also, arriving slowly. Everything was yet to be arranged. A truck is going to look for some trumpets. We are given chairs on the veranda of the Territory. And there we wait and wait. About nine o'clock, there is a little animation. They are going to get Gbenye (who had already arrived at five o'clock this morning) with a cart. When he finally arrives and comes among us, there is a big parade with all the schools and soldiers participating and lots of fanfare. So around ten o'clock, three speeches are given by the notables of Bondo, and then Gbenye gives his speech. That went on for an hour and a half! At first he spoke in French, then in Lingala. He began with a short history of the Congo: the primitive times (the Europeans had also known such a period); the period of slavery; and then the colonization (a camouflaged form of slavery); and finally independence, which was now threatened by the moves made by Kasavubu and his crowd who were selling the country to the imperialist Americans, the Belgians, the Chinese, and the Russians. The fact that he faulted China and Russia surprised us. Finally, it seems from all this that they don't want to submit to any communist influence. After that, Gbenye addressed himself more and more to us, the fathers. He gave an exposé in favor of freedom of religion. He was a Catholic, even though he didn't practice any longer. But he didn't want, as a Catholic, to impose his faith on the population. Since he was a Catholic, he should respect and live his religion, for example in marriage, he should have only one wife. A Mohammedan might have three wives. That was fine. A pagan could stay a pagan and have as many wives as he wanted. Each one should respect the other. And then, he began all of a sudden to speak of the indigenous fetishism, which had a lot of good in it and so it should be used. It's God who gave these powers to nature and to men. Then he spoke of judgments of the Church: one cannot condemn it and its ministers. When a priest is bad, that doesn't mean that the Church is bad. Then, he paid homage to us: we had not taken flight as so many others had. Bondo was the only locality where he had been well received by the whites...Bondo was the head of all for all in the province. The public applauded at this point. At Buta, where he had studied with the Marist Brothers, everybody had taken flight. He didn't want to condemn them, but yet he found that it was not right. Even when one is afraid, where is the love of the martyr?

It was around eleven thirty that everything was over and that we noticed how many people were really there: all the roads were full of people...The Simba drove the sisters back in a car. The rapport between us and the population was very good. After the political meeting, the different groups were able to ask for an audience with Gbenye. Father Jan van Wagenberg and the diocesan priest Father Jean went up to him to thank him for the welcome at Stanleyville and also for the money that he had returned. We don't think that he should be thanked since he only did his duty. He tried to place some cars at our disposal. But he remarked that formerly the missionaries went everywhere on foot and that worked out very well. They were practically heroes. And now the situation had changed. He noted that there were fewer miracles. He had need of something to help him hobble around...

Brother Lambert has not yet returned from Baye. A grade-school principal informs us that a lot actually has been stolen in Baye: typewriters, clothes, shoes, etc.

Sunday, October 18

Today is the canonization of the martyrs of Uganda: a great day for the African Church. We don't even announce it in church because we fear the same sort of difficulties that we had last week, when we had announced the death of Monsignor Daniel.

This morning, Brother Lambert was at the center of our curious confreres; he came back to Bondo yesterday evening. What he recounts is hardly comforting: on the road to Baye, the Simba acted yet as they had here before our departure for Stanleyville. At the mission of the Crosiers, everything has been looted, even the washbasins and the statues of the Virgin. There are still some tables. The mattresses are there yet. It wasn't much better at the sisters'. Whereas at the brothers' everything was yet intact, except for the cows that had been stolen. In the evening, a Simba tells us that Gbenye is here in the region so that he can flee as quickly as possible…Even though probably nothing of this is true, it shows a certain mentality among these men. (It's typical: Gbenye had said that he was ready to die, and that the flight of the chief of state to another country is not cowardly but a benediction for his people.)

Monday, October 19

Today, Father Filip Waldram learns from a sure source that the soldiers have installed their camp at the mission of the Crosiers and the sisters at Monga. That means a complete pillaging. They were first set up at the mission of the Protestants, on the mountain, but that was too high for them.

Brother Lambert went to the Territory today to make a report. They will try to return everything and send some soldiers up there to arrest some of the hyper Simba.

At noon, everybody is obliged to go to the mission: our new commander has need to scold us.

When we all have arrived, he began his speech, but that finished in nothing flat. He called the diocesan priest Father Jean to come up before everybody and he asked from whom and where he had received his education. Everybody answered: "With us." That finished, he looked at the point on his shoes and began to laugh in a silly manner and in an incoherent way said that he also was at Stanleyville during the agitations and our kidnapping, but that was a fact of orders received and that finally all was over now. If we had anything to complain about, we could begin immediately. Once again, it was necessary to compile a list of things stolen. We could then get going. Nobody knew exactly what he was talking about by this "performance," but it was evident that he meant to make amends for the past.

A Belgian of the C.V.C. who came to have a cup of coffee with us says that there is indeed an important grouping of the

National Congolese Army at Bumba: four airplanes, a lot of military equipment and supplies, five hundred soldiers, and forty mercenaries. According to what he says, it's from that side that our liberation will come: Bumba, Aketi, and afterward Buta and Bondo.

Tuesday, October 20

Last night, around midnight, the three Capuchin fathers[20] from Yakoma, who were always at Buta, have arrived here in Bondo. They had to leave Buta. Why? They don't know. Our three confreres[21] stayed there with the American doctor from Yakoma. This was best. At Buta it is peaceful, as here. Gbenye did not have a better reception anywhere than here. The three Capuchins will stay here temporarily, for there is no question of a return to Monga and to Yakoma.

After dinner, Brother Lambert and Father Jef Beckers left for Baye with some Simba to put everything in order there.

Wednesday, October 21

At noon we receive good news: Radio Brussels announces that the fathers from Bumba arrived in Leopoldville and there made a complete report of the situation: how we all had to make the trip to Stanleyville, that it had come about from an error, and that everybody was in good health. They spoke of each group in particular: the Capuchins from Yakoma, the Crosiers from Bondo, and the Premonstratensians from Buta. And so, it's in this way that we learn that we are all still living.

Thursday, October 22

A peaceful day. The confreres have not yet returned from Baye.

Friday, October 23

The confreres who went to Baye have still not returned. The communications coming from Monga and from Lobi are more and more serious. Even the school materials have been destroyed.

Some interesting news has been communicated by Radio Brussels: the bishop, the fathers, and the sisters from Lolo were able

20 Fathers Monulf Schrijvers, Leopold Nijvens, and Adriaan vanden Brouke

21 Father Polydoor Carremans and Brothers Egbert Mensink and Leonard Rooyakkers, who were liberated at Buta on November 25, 1964, and were able to return immediately to Europe

to flee to Bumba even though they were not yet liberated. They are then in security. We will be then the last ones…

Saturday, October 24

At eleven o'clock, the diocesan priest Father Jean arrives by bike from the seminary to give us this sensational news: Aketi has been taken! If this is true, the radio will quickly give us some certainty. A truck has come back from Baye with some Simba aboard who are tied up: they are the ones who directed the pillage. Father Beckers and Brother Lambert stayed up there. There are piles of stuff from the mission in the truck; everything has to be taken to the Territory for the inquest and will be returned afterward.

During dinner the new commander comes to ask for a Requiem Mass for a lieutenant from Buta who was killed in a car accident. He was very friendly and polite. After dinner, Brother Stanislaus Verschueren shares the contents of a speech that Gbenye broadcasted on Radio Stanleyville. He said, among other things, that he had arrested an American major at Yakoma last September 20 and that he was going to judge him now at Stanleyville. We think that it is certainly the doctor from Yakoma. He added that he was leaving the whites in peace and that when he was on his trip through the region of the Uele, he found that everything there was peaceful.

A grade-school teacher from Lobi, whose car had been destroyed by the Simba, came to report it at Bondo; at the same time, he made a report of the looting of the buildings of the mission. This was certainly a courageous guy.

In the evening: Brother Lambert and Father Beckers came back from Baye. Up there, in the meantime, more had been stolen. Some rooms were practically empty. It seems that all this was due to the Youth rather than the real soldiers. Some of the things stolen from Baye are now here, at Bondo.

We learn some details about the communiqué concerning Aketi. After the fall of Bumba, the Simba had initiated another attack, but they were pushed back from Bumba; the National Congolese Army pursued them within about twenty miles from Aketi.

Radio Coquilhatville announces that Boende fell this morning at eleven thirty. This is getting very interesting!

Today, three trucks were brought here to take the Simba from Bondo to the front at Yakoma. They refused to go!

Sunday, October 25, the Feast of Christ the King

This morning, there were still some Simba at the High Mass, among them some chiefs, dressed as civilians this time.

Also this morning, I heard the history of part of the life of our very friendly commander Vincent. Before the "war" he was a businessman at Buta. As the result of serious dysentery, he was hospitalized and taken care of by the sisters. At the time when he left the hospital, it was noticed that a whole pile of stuff had disappeared. They knew who to suspect, of that there was no doubt, and so Vincent was put in prison. He was freed by the rebels and began his military career. He himself admitted to the sisters that he had stolen...

We always eat at the mission: *"un skon toafel mi volk"*[22] the folks at Uden would say. This had been the cause of some worry to Brother Willem. For a few weeks now, there has not been enough potatoes. There's always less meat, but that will get better perhaps, since there's still some cattle at Baye. What we're missing is some beer, for which we've forgotten the taste a long time ago. Fortunately, since our trip to Stanleyville, there are plenty of cigarettes.

In the end, we can't complain too much, despite the uncertainty of the moment and of the "way" we will be freed.

Monday, October 26

Radio Coquilhatville announced, yesterday evening, that all the missionaries of Boende were in good health.

Today, the Solemn Requiem Mass was celebrated for the lieutenant of Buta. There were a lot of people there for the Mass, which began forty-five minutes late. It was only after three-quarters of an hour that we heard the singing of the soldiers arriving who assisted at the Mass. A string of soldiers took up position on the principal road where the authorities arrive, one of whom is an extraordinary provincial commissary who arrived yesterday evening.

22 Dutch in the Uden dialect: "the feeling of home with friends around the table." The Crosiers have had a house and school in Uden for several centuries, and the author, Father Jan Verhoeven, was himself from Uden.

All the fathers, brothers, and sisters were present. A lot of school kids also. The sounding of trumpets during the consecration was so off-key that I will never forget it.

After the Mass, there was a gathering with a parade in honor of the newly arrived big shot. Yet another time we endure the same boring program: we wait a whole hour and then Mr. Louis arrives (that's his name), then the parade is followed by some speeches. His was short, simple, and good. He gives the impression of not being a bad guy. He presents himself as a man who is coming to reestablish order both at the level of administration as well as that of the military.

We whites were again praised and appreciation was expressed for us once again, and the most complete security was promised us for as long as we abstain from any political intervention. The children and the workers received a free day, and then it was over. We were very well treated during the whole program: we were immediately shown to some chairs and we were amiably treated by all those who had something to say.

When you attend such a gathering, you wonder about these guys who act as if nothing is wrong, yet at the same time they are increasingly becoming entrapped.

Once we got back home, we heard a new sampling of "*mayle na mondele*," a white trick! Father (Hendrik) Verberk of Monga had had to give his watch to a Simba (an automatic Pontiac). Here in Bondo, the Simba wanted to sell it, and a white bought it, for he was thinking such a beautiful watch probably belonged to one of the fathers. He brought it over today and wouldn't accept a cent for it. A very friendly act on his part.

At noon: According to Radio Brussels, the National Congolese Army is going toward Aketi and then heading for Stanleyville. Are they going to forget us here?

At four o'clock: A Mercedes arrives at the seminary. The commissary is a former seminarian, and he comes another time to pay us a visit. The first impressions of this morning prove to be right on: he is a very friendly man and very peaceful. He leaves after a visit. He was also at the sisters' and at the mission where he was informed of various things. Tomorrow the diocesan priest Father Jean-Pierre will try to go with him to Monga.

Tuesday, October 27

Father Jean-Pierre was not able to leave with the extraordinary commissary, for they say they had need of the car to get ammunition at Buta: they are preparing for punitive measures against the population of Muma. If that's true, it's a frightful thing!

During the evening hours: There's a lot of talk about the news according to which there were some deaths among the missionaries and the white businessmen at Boende and at Katako-Kombe. Such news does nothing for the atmosphere here. Besides, we are always waiting, playing cards, reading, and discussing, all of which gets tiring. Despite the danger that it represents, we would all love for the National Congolese Army to attack Bondo this evening.

Wednesday, October 28

Just after breakfast, we saw a truck loaded with soldiers take off. For Yakoma? Or for Monga, where it seems the situation is desperate. Radio Brussels announces at noon: fifteen of eighteen missionaries (among whom were four sisters) of Boende arrived yesterday in Brussels; the three others remain biding their time at Coquilhatville. At noon, we heard a discourse from the general on the radio: if Tshombe continues to recruit the whites[23] he will do it also. He would leave the whites in peace, but, at the least sign of political activity, they will be killed. In the meantime, news arrives concerning a formation of planes that flew over Aketi and are continuing in the direction of Likati. The tension mounts again: tonight, one of the whites passed the whole night on his bed, all dressed and ready to go. Today, Brother Lambert departed again for Baye to get some cows, among other things.

According to Radio Leopoldville, three whites were killed at Boende. In the evening some terrible stories about Monga are reported to us: some women and young girls have been raped, and the worst kind of anarchy reigns in Monga.

---

23 These are white mercenaries under General Mike Hoare who led the Congolese army against the Simba rebels. Hoare's book, *Congo Mercenary*, was published by Robert Hale of London in 1967. When they marched on Buta at the end of May, it was detected by the rebels, and hence, they arrived two days too late.

N. B. The diary is taken up again on October 30 at noon. Since Wednesday night to Thursday and up to Friday noon, we were again put under arrest. I will try to give you the essentials of this episode.

During the night I was awakened by blows on my door; it was around twelve thirty in the morning. It was Father Godfried Kraewinkels, who quickly closed the door behind him. He said he heard a vehicle and then blows on the door. We are there a few seconds, when there is another knocking at the door. It's the diocesan priest Father Jerome, who says that we have to depart immediately. We have to take our blankets and some pillows and get into a truck. We ask the reason for it. All he knows is that a telegram has arrived from Stanleyville and all of us are to be lodged in a big empty house. We gather together a few things and head for the truck, while soldiers are walking all over the place. We notice that they are particularly calm, they don't hit us, they only ask us to hurry up. The other fathers and brothers are already next to the vehicle. They show us the telegram. The Belgians; the fathers, brothers, and sisters; and the Americans are summoned to a house arrest, for they have seen Belgians and Americans with airplanes. It's also noted that they may not hit the whites, which explains their calm manner. During the night, we go through Bondo in the truck, and after several trips, we are all taken to the empty house of the doctor. Of all the whites, only the Belgians are present. The Protestant missionaries are here also, with their wives. Slowly, we calm down and find a little rest, even on the floor.

Thursday, October 29

Some of us were able to sleep. Most of us simply just lay down, with nothing else happening. In the morning we try to clarify the situation a little. Of the businessmen, they only brought along the Belgians. Why the Crosiers, the brothers, and the Dutch sisters? Why the Norwegian Protestants? And moreover, we were badly lodged; it wasn't very comfortable. The house is found in the prolongation of the dock for the ferry. It's the first house that you see on arriving in Bondo. Our situation would be far from desirable if the National Congolese Army were to attack Bondo. Is this what they want? Some are able to depart to prepare some sandwiches. At ten thirty, we are able to eat a little. The ambiance and the appetite are not the best. A little later, the brothers who work in the garage are able to go, and one sister is able to go to the hospital. They all have to come back in the evening. In the meantime, we learn that the women at the hospital would like to come and protest as do the pupils at the normal school who are held back by a black brother.

The Simba and some of the heads of the rebellion regularly come "to look at us." We ask them for some explanations. They say that they have again sent a telegram to find out what to do. We only have to wait. We hope also for the intervention of the extraordinary commissary, who ought to be already back from Monga. A telegram arrives from Stanleyville: it says that all the foreigners should remain under arrest; that classes should be terminated; that the Americans were in the process of assassinating the Congolese; but that they, the rebels, wouldn't do such a thing. We are expecting then that they will round up all the whites, but they don't do anything. On the contrary, the Protestants are able to return home after having proven that they were Norwegians. This happens before the arrival of the second telegram. That gave a great hope to our group, the Dutch. But we had the impression that they were hesitating when we presented our passports because there were so many of us with Dutch passports.

In the course of the afternoon, we have the certainty of passing a second night on the same floor. It's for this reason that we had brought to us, besides some food, some rubber mattresses and some pillows.

Our guards were very friendly and forbade the other Simba to come and make fun of us. We were able to freely walk around the house outside and even to go as far as the Uele to wash.

We went to bed fairly early (we naturally did not have lighting except a small kerosene lamp that attracted hordes of mosquitoes). Most of us sleep at least until midnight. Then we are awakened by some Simba who sing and talk as loud as possible behind the house. You get the sense that they are smoking marijuana. Everything that they sang and said was against us; what they said was often dirty and gross. Marijuana must provoke the baser instincts for we met these same guys during the day and they were very friendly. They go to sleep about one o'clock. And so do we!

Friday, October 30

The day begins, and several of us go down to wash in the Uele. That feels good. After an orange and a banana (the black sisters and the mission house boys bring us all sorts of things to eat) several Crosiers begin to play cards. They stop it fairly quickly, for there is a lot to observe today. This morning, we were awakened by some gunshots on the other side of the Uele, and someone among us says that it could announce the arrival of the commander of Buta, Augustine Makondo, who had a partiality for the command "Fire!" Our confrere was not mistaken. And the commander was followed by five or six trucks full of soldiers. Everybody passed over the river and assembled around the flag. There were at least a thousand Simba. This was not reassuring to see. They were harangued by the commander. They must go to participate in the combat at Yakoma. If they refused to go or tried to flee, they would be shot in the back.

In the hours that followed, we saw the coming and going of trucks, jeeps, and cars. One had rarely seen so much traffic in Bondo. Some Simba passed by us and looked at us, but there were only a few who were not able to refrain from spitting out their hate at us. *Toward noon*, it began to rain. Then the commander of Bondo, Basil, suggested to us that he himself would go in his car to get us something to eat.

This Basil has hardly showed us a favorable day thus far, but it's getting better. On the other hand, the fact that he goes to get our food signifies that we are going to stay here. We were hoping to return home, for we had introduced a proposal, which seemed to be fairly well received; if we were under "house arrest" we could just as well stay home and be assembled in the dormitory of the seminary. There were a hundred beds, the hall was large and was close to the bathroom and sinks, and (but we didn't say this) we would have more security than here next to the Uele. Another commander arrived during the meal, and we brought up this subject to him. He was in complete agreement with us and promised us to work on this right away. We hadn't finished eating and two trucks arrived. This commander acted on his ideas promptly. We were able to load up our things.

We ourselves had to await the arrival of the commander, Augustine. What excitement! The commander arrived a little later. We obtained permission to depart and even more. Each one of us could go to his own room. Nevertheless, we would be under "house arrest." We could celebrate a Mass, but for the rest we had to stay in our rooms. They seem to have forgotten the bit about the dormitory.

So now we are again at home as if nothing had happened, except that our anxiety has grown. Now, we really are in the thick of things. We can't reopen our schools: we are afraid that the airplanes might mix up our students with the Simba. So, everybody has gone home, except for one Protestant who's lodging at the seminary. I haven't yet spied one soldier who might be guarding us. I went by bike over to the brothers' house, for an evening Mass, without any ambushes. A little later, we learned that some of the officers (one of whom is the commander Vincent) were not in agreement as to how we had been treated. One of them said: "They treated you like pigs."

Now, we are waiting again to see how all this unfolds. The commander Vincent came to see us at the mission, and he whispered to us: "In fact, I would like to drive you in two trucks to Bangassou, but I cannot do it." And then he added: "I myself would like to flee."

In the evening: Brother Lambert has come back from Baye. He experienced some pretty crazy things, but in the end, he is home safe and sound along with four cows. It should be noticed that there wasn't one soldier with a rifle to kill these animals when he was looking for the cows. He himself had to sedate them and shoot them.

In the meantime, Father Filip Waldram has obtained the latest news on the situation at Monga by intermediary of the principal of the grade school and the diocesan priests. Things couldn't be worse.

The extraordinary commissary, himself originally from Monga, was furious. He was so ashamed that he couldn't even come to see us and say "hello" before his return to Stanleyville. Monga might as well be burned down: there's nothing left to loot. Even at the church. They even threw the chasubles around. The population has nothing left. All those who had a halfway decent house were preyed upon because they had certainly bought it with money from RADECO (the outlawed political party).

Eleven Simba were made prisoners. Those who remained would be replaced by others. According to information received, things haven't been any better at Lobi.

At quarter to nine: A truck full of unfriendly soldiers abruptly enters the mission...All of us have to go to the dormitory. They're going along anyway it seems with our original proposal. Everything happens without warning. You see everywhere the Crosiers transporting some mattresses and blankets. The soldiers are very suspicious: if you go into your room for one thing or another, one of them accompanies you. They profit by the occasion to ask for watches and clothes. Several of the soldiers are drunk. Mr. Godin, who was sleeping already in one of the bedrooms of the seminary, is torn from his bed and led to the dormitory. His wife, who was with him, has to go to the sisters' house. Basil seems again to be directing operations. They go to get the brothers also. For ten hours, we are all together. It's in the presence of serious guards that the night begins (three Simba survey us in the dorm and block the doors). Their severity diminished somewhat when the chief left, and I did some physical exercises to show that I indeed was the teacher of gymnastics at the seminary.

Saturday, October 31

In the morning, walking in formation, we quietly go to the church. Most of us were still in the church, when suddenly there is some shooting and we all have to rapidly return to the mission. What's new? It seems that it wasn't anything: the commander Augustine wanted to test his guards at the gates, and so he fired with his machine gun without showing himself. The reaction: the Simba threw off their arms and battle equipment and took flight in the woods. Now they are all in jail.

So we eat at the mission and then return to the recreation room at the seminary: we play checkers, cards, read, and...wait.

Via a Congolese Brother of Saint Gabriel, Pierre, we receive some news from Paulis. It has to be bad down there. Today, Brother Lambert departed for Baye with two sisters to get some more cows. Some fathers and brothers can go to the mission, under escort, to kill and butcher two cows. Brother Peerke, who assists at the "operation," is a little sad: one of the cows slain was the best of the stable, giving twenty-six gallons a week, which is a lot for the Congo.

Sunday, November 1, All Saints

Peaceful night. Some of these rascals are in the church during the High Mass. After, we return directly to the recreation room. It's calm until just after benediction. Then, it's the noise of battle: a lot of gunshots. A mortar hits.

Gbenye speaks on the radio: since the African states refuse to help, he will apply the politics of burnt land. The evening is calm and pleasant; our guards play cards with us.

Monday, November 2, All Souls

Another peaceful night. At eight o'clock in the morning, the solemn funeral of Monsignor Daniel Katosi. The radio announces: from Boende they have progressed within three hundred miles of Stanleyville. Our famous Basil has fled. The one who finds him can shoot him immediately.

Our guards today are a little more severe. In the afternoon, Brother Marcel is invited to coffee with the commander Augustine.

Tuesday, November 3

Because we have plenty of time, we celebrate a Conventual Mass.[24] Afterward, they come to get Father Marinus Godefrooy: he has to go to Baye to print some cards for them. They depart after dinner in two cars that are held together only by a miracle.

After coffee, the lieutenant Vincent brings us a camera. It must belong to Father Jan van Oort. He will also bring us some tape decks, he says.

And then the usual day of those held captive: read; play chess, checkers, and cards; and pray. This evening, for the first time, the tape deck plays some happy music for us.

In the evening: They bring a white from the C.V.C. of Likati, Jean de Strooper. He was in prison for six days. We had known him before. In the evening also, the two fathers who went to the printing press

24 A Conventual Mass is the community Mass. It's probably the day of prayer for deceased confreres of the Order. Normally, confreres would also celebrate a personal Mass with a server, as was the custom before the introduction of concelebration by Vatican II.

at Baye come back; they were unable to cross the Gangu-Bili River because of the water level.

During evening recreation, one of the chiefs comes to bother us; we had to stop the tape deck. He counts us, and then after some scoldings, he goes away.

Our Simba guardians tell us that Aketi was bombed and that the consequences were heavy: twenty whites were killed and four hundred natives. A little later, we learn that one white had been beaten to death and that eight bombs had actually been dropped over Aketi.

Wednesday, November 4

This morning, we learned that they had awakened the sisters yesterday evening, for the purpose of counting them. We received other news from Aketi: the soldiers there wanted to attack the white women, but the authorities were able to restrain them. They come to tell Father Filip Waldram of Monga that there are some things from Monga at the Territory. We will go tomorrow to see.

Thursday, November 5

The sisters also came to the Conventual Mass, which today was a votive Mass for peace.

The guards have become friendlier; we are "on vacation" and we're able to go to the showers or to our rooms. We receive some disquieting news from the environs of Boende: a superior was murdered, and two fathers and two sisters were kidnapped.

Fathers Filip Waldram and Albert Timmers come back about ten thirty from the office at the Territory. What they were able to find of the things stolen from Monga was disappointing; they amounted to a small statue, a pair of sandals, and some coat hangers.

At the Territory, they were witnesses of a typical happening: a Simba who had been wounded at Yakoma and who had been able to escape by jumping in the river had to explain how he was able to do it. He had to reveal to them his "miraculous" secret. Since he wasn't able to do it, he was thrown into prison.

At noon: It is horribly hot in the dormitory.

In the evening: A bolt of lightning struck us by way of the radio:

Monga has been taken; the population enthusiastically welcomed the National Congolese Army.

Friday, November 6

Most of us slept badly this past night, after the news of yesterday evening. Several people kept their clothes on. We're hardly hungry this morning. The tension is very high.

This makes three months that this sad situation exists here. It goes on and on. The sisters come again to the Conventual Mass; they had not known anything about the fall of Monga.

During the day, the radio confirms again the news about Monga. The mood is not one of the best. We're afraid.

At noon: It is communicated that Kindu has fallen. There's one thing that we do not understand: why the peace reigns always at Bondo. To see the Simba, you wouldn't suspect anything. Our logical conclusion is that they would like to surrender and that they're waiting peacefully for their enemy.

In the evening: The commander Augustine comes to play cards. Nothing betrays his thoughts. Some already doubt the communications on the subject of Monga. Brother Willem tells us that Tshombe has launched an appeal by radio for all to put down their arms. According to what he says, Stanleyville, Paulis, and Bambessa will be ready to surrender. Those who surrender voluntarily will save their lives.

Saturday, November 7

The mood is one of hope and a certain optimism. It's very warm. Some chiefs come to look for shorts for football. Everything gives the impression that, indeed, they will surrender. The fathers of Baye have not returned.

Sunday, November 8

The day begins badly: after Mass, we speak with some youth who have come back from Monga…There's nothing going on there. So the news on the radio is then false. The mood goes down quickly.

At noon, some young whites arrive; the commander is inviting us to a football match with the Simba. We quickly accept even though we discuss whether it wouldn't be better, for our security, to let the Simba win...

After dinner: A new uncertainty. One of the diocesan priests believes that the youth who pretended to be coming back from Monga were not really there; it was a question of Simba who were put up to this at Bondo. Some news of the doctor of Yakoma has arrived: he's freely attending to his affairs at Stanleyville. This is good news!

They come to get the football players in a truck at five o'clock. They come to get the other Crosiers as well. The field is in good condition. The seats are occupied by the military and civil authorities. There are a lot of people, especially Simba. Our team is composed of the Crosiers, the two diocesan priests, and some Europeans. Our superiors have the right to places of honor. A terrific comedy, such as is not possible but here. The majority of the public support the whites.

We arrive at halftime with the score 2 to 0 in our favor. During the pause, we are offered some Coca-Cola. For the big shots, there's some beer. Thanks to the great playing by the diocesan priests, the whites win 4 to 1.

After the match, the two teams line up in front of the stands. The administrator of the Territory cries out "Long live the Europeans!" Then, they take us back to our camp of internment. Enthusiasm reigns. We think now for sure that there's a plan of surrender; this won't last longer than a few more days. We have survived it all well.

In the evening: The two fathers return from Baye. They had passed through a whole mess of irritating things and were happy to be again with us. According to what they say, the others are already at Lobi...at Baye there were Simba who didn't dare return to Bondo.

Monday, November 9

The invitation of a functionary of the state to Father Filip Waldram to accompany him to Monga plunges us into wonderment...Is there nothing going on there? Or do they play this game of deception in a masterful way? A little later, we learn that the commander has requisitioned all the native rifles. The Simba are to return all their arms. Is this a favorable sign? We don't understand anything anymore. Father Marinus Godefrooy receives twelve thousand francs for his printing work.

Tuesday, November 10

Everything is peaceful, except there are a few gunshots in the morning. At noon, one of the house boys of Lobi comes to see us and to give a report on the situation down there. Everything was looted and destroyed, even in the sacristy. Even the refrigerator was demolished. According to him there are still a lot of Simba at Lobi and at Monga. After dinner, there is a communication that General Olenga was assassinated. He would've been the one in charge of the fall of Kindu.

Even better news now: Radio Leopoldville has literally announced yesterday evening that a column of the National Congolese Army would march on Bondo from Monga. We begin to believe it, for one of the youth who wanted to go back to Monga did not receive permission.

In the evening: The commander of Lobi comes in here mouthing off. Snarling at Father Filip Waldram, he demands a battery. Then he screams that he wants the generator going all night, because tomorrow morning all the batteries are to be charged up. We are all agitated by the time we go to bed.

Wednesday, November 11

An official decree announces that no one can go to Monga because they are repairing a bridge. Many of us don't believe any of it; we think it's a question of a new excuse in not wanting anyone to go in that direction. What should we think of it?

Thursday, November 12

The sisters always come to the Conventual Mass. The guards are friendly. It's a little less hot today.

Friday, November 13

During the early hours of the morning, there are remarkably fewer people in the streets. A kind of judge has come from Stanleyville to speak to Father Jan van Wagenberg for any information on the subject of Basil. No news from the front.

In bringing us some tangerines, Brother Pierre also brings along this news: the National Congolese Army is supposed to be six miles from Stanleyville. After the affair with Monga, we no longer believe any communications. In the course of the morning, we receive a letter from Brother Jef of Bili. Everything is going well there and also at Ango. They also are under house arrest. He also writes that the ferryboat at Api has been demolished. After the siesta, Mr. Garcia (a resident of Bondo) comes to say that the National Congolese Army is certainly not at Monga: one of the most trustworthy of men has just come from there.

In the evening, Brother Willem brings us some more news: According to the brother of the spy of Bondo, everything will be finished here in Bondo before December 3.

Saturday, November 14

This evening more news hits us: the doctor of Yakoma will be judged at Stanleyville as a major of the American Army. They will wait for the execution until there is some response from America. The fathers of Yakoma are especially affected by this news.

Sunday, November 15

Nothing special. A good Sunday to sleep!

Monday, November 16

The black sister postulants will probably leave today. They are afraid to stay here at Bondo. Moreover, it seems like a lot of people are going away. Our commander Augustine is named a major.

Around six o'clock, there is a communication that the doctor of Yakoma will be executed within two hours. Terrible. Our mood, which had been better after the first part of the volleyball game, now falls back to zero.

In the evening: We learn that the execution will take place tonight.

Tuesday, November 17

The mission, where we all go to eat, is seeing some Simba arrive more and more. It appears that they consider it like a hotel, they ask to eat and for a bed. Each day there are more of them, and almost all the visitors' rooms are taken. Some women come in the evening and leave in the morning. There's nothing that you can do about it. Just a little before eleven o'clock, the sisters bring big news: Stanleyville has been taken. A Portuguese woman had brought the news to them, trembling all the while. Is it true? Two whites come afterward to say that Aketi will also be taken. Father Willem Vissers should accompany the black postulants of the sisters to Bili today, but at the last minute, there's naturally not one truck available.

The last news: Dulia and Aketi have been bombed. We take it as a big joke.

In the evening: We organize again a volleyball match.

Wednesday, November 18

Tonight, we were awakened at midnight by a lot of shooting that went on for a long time. This morning, it seems that Augustine (who has just become a major) has come back.

After breakfast, a member of the parish council of Monga brings us news from up there. Everything that he reports is horrible news: according to his story all the villages along the Uele have been burned. At Monga itself, the Simba had drunk beer from the chalices of the church. Later in the day, we learn that the execution of the doctor of Yakoma has been delayed indefinitely. We are happy about it. It appears that the whole world has been moved by the news of the execution.

A telegram arrived from Stanleyville says that the Simba can no longer ride around during the night. The fall of Stanleyville was evidently false news…

Thursday, November 19

Immediately after breakfast, three fathers leave in an open jeep with the major. There are two trips planned: the printing press at Baye for Father Willem Vissers and a trip to Bili and Ango.

We celebrate a sung Conventual Mass again. They work from morning to night. It seems that they are occupied in making a sort of bomb, probably in imitation of the Molotov cocktails that were used in Budapest. Indeed, they promise a car for Father Willem, but two fathers leave first for Baye. Gbenye announced, on the radio, that if Stanleyville is attacked, all the Belgians and all the Americans will be killed. The execution of the doctor of Yakoma is fixed for next Monday.

Radio Stanleyville: the population is wild! They are asking for all the whites so that they can eat them…General Opepe has presented his resignation.

A white from Bondo, who was sick, has been able to leave for Bangassou. He's taking our telegrams for Europe.

Friday, November 20

The National Congolese Army is within twenty-eight miles of Stanleyville. Some Belgian senators have arrived in Leopoldville to treat this desperate situation at Stanleyville.

At four o'clock: Five hundred Belgian troops, who arrived by parachute, are already on the Island of Saint Helen, ready to liberate the whites of Stanleyville. The tension is going up here. In the meantime, many Simba from here have left for the front at Muma.

Saturday, November 21

Little news, so one constructs all sorts of troubling hypotheses and difficulties.

Sunday, November 22

Two soldiers come from the front, and they recount, among other things, that Augustine killed on the spot a soldier who fired at the population.

Monday, November 23

In the morning, Brother Pierre comes to announce that they probably will requisition all radios. They were already occupied at the other whites' houses. We quickly hide some of ours.

It is announced to us that a telegram has arrived from Stanleyville ordering the reopening of all the schools…This is incredible, considering that the situation is so…explosive.

In the evening: The pastor of Bili arrives here. The stories of horror are beginning again, though, for the moment, things are going fairly well down there. The execution of the doctor is postponed until the negotiations on December 2.

TUESDAY, NOVEMBER 24

I go again to celebrate Mass at the brothers' house. You don't see many people in the streets. On coming back home, I learn that there is a sort of an "alert" today. They are waiting for an attack against Aketi.

The automobile traffic is intense. The sisters don't come to the Conventual Mass.

A little later: "they" will already be at Aketi, and "ours" here prepare their retreat.

The diocesan priest Father Jean-Pierre comes to tell us that Leopoldville has declared that Stanleyville has been taken. The Belgian troops are there.

N. B. The diary is taken up again on November 26.

Around ten thirty in the morning on November 24, a truck full of loud-mouthed soldiers arrives. They invade our hall. Each of us has to immediately take off his habit. Father Huub van Lieshout has only his shorts on...We have to quickly put other clothes on and we are on our way. The greatest panic reigns among us. They drive us to a new residence where we are under house arrest, in a house near the Uele. All the whites are "penned" up this time, the children and the old folks as well. There are eighty of us. Confusion and fear...At a certain moment, when everybody is inside, all the windows must be closed. Somebody faints. We have to hand over all our watches and glasses. Then, an "angel" arrives who puts an end to this comedy. The windows and the doors can be opened. They give back some glasses. At noon, some people are able to go back home. The sisters are also able to return. We stay. After a rather meager meal, the night begins: not much room and only a few blankets.

WEDNESDAY, NOVEMBER 25

Feeling like we have lumbago, we get up, leaving behind the cold planks. Meanwhile, we learn the big news: Stanleyville is really taken.

Eight hundred whites have been evacuated. Major Augustine comes at noon. He looks very tired. He says, as far as we are concerned, "you are not at fault." We are expecting that we will be able to go home today. Actually, the mechanics from the garage can go; and also Father Frans Waldram who is ill; our superior, Father Jan van Wagenberg; and Brother Peerke. We begin a second night with more space and more blankets.

Thursday, November 26

News in the morning: Buta has also been taken. The tension mounts among us. After some time, Augustine comes to get Father Vissers. A little afterward, we learn that Father Vissers gave Augustine a million francs to pay the soldiers. They are going to flee, he says. A little later, we can go home. The mood is exuberant. The war is over.

Back home, we learn that the doctor of Yakoma was killed. There were moreover many dead and wounded among the whites of the population. We all go back to our hall. And again, it's panic that reigns. If all those who have a little authority take flight, that could be a more dangerous situation. Soldiers in flight can do anything. Our big problem is: where will we go? What will we do if some group tries to take us along? In the dormitory we collect some clubs and other "arms," just in case…The brothers go back home. There, they can easily take flight in the forest, they say. Some of us try to calm down the others.

The afternoon is more peaceful. We decide not to celebrate an evening Mass. During the night, we take turns keeping guard.

Radio Paris, this evening: The Belgian paratroops have also come to Paulis. We learn also that some women have constructed a barricade to keep back the Simba who are fleeing.

At eight o'clock: Four guards arrive. Some students who should be staying with us can go back home. Haven't they taken flight yet?

The night begins. Will they come tonight? The fathers of Baye are still there and don't know anything of what's going on.

Friday, November 27

Upon awakening, everything is peaceful. Our guards are there and many Simba have stayed in Bondo. We celebrate a community

Mass, during which each one goes to communion. Brother Pierre reports that at Paulis where his family lives, four thousand people have been assassinated, among them some whites.

Some official letters on the subject of the death of Monsignor Daniel Katosi arrive at noon.

At quarter to four: the two fathers came back from Baye. Everybody is happy. They met with many difficulties and spent a night in prison, but in the end all is okay.

In bringing the coffee, Brother Lambert brings along also some tragic-comic news; he went peacefully to see where the brothers (of Saint Gabriel) were, and he found them in the forest. They had dug themselves in under a cover in waiting for some cars that were passing by.

Mrs. Godin comes to announce that she has spoken with one of the "patrons" who is still here. He speaks about surrender and protection of the whites if we protect them also.

Saturday, November 28

Augustine has killed another Simba, and another was mortally wounded by a grenade. It could happen that there will develop a reaction against him, and that could be dangerous for us.

At noon: We learn that two whites have been imprisoned. What does that signify? They are Belgians. Since our return, all the sisters are with us, and they will stay here until the liberation. The parrot of Sister Eunodia entertains everybody by his idiotic remarks.

At four thirty: Major Augustine comes to say that all the sisters must return to their respective domiciles. They should not be afraid. We are to remain here.

At six thirty: A luxurious car arrives all of a sudden, and, without commentary, the two white laymen who are with us have to leave immediately: Mr. Godin and Jean de Strooper. They cannot even get a coat or sweater. The soldiers are brutal.

At eight o'clock: The commander enters, helping Mrs. Godin. He puts down his gun and falls to his knees. We all gather around him. He is in a strange mood, and Mrs. Godin is pale as death. He begins to pray and to tell us how he had taken her into the forest in order to seduce her. She refused. Then he said that he would kill her. She asked for time to pray. That made such an impression on him that he decided to spare her.

We listen to all this with amazement. He had smoked some marijuana. He speaks of a martyr and of death. He speaks of the Holy Spirit and of God the Father. He finishes by asking for a prayer for himself and for Mrs. Godin.

Then he gives a pile of money to our guards while telling them with fervor that they should treat us well. He goes away alone in the middle of the night. Mrs. Godin is there, in a chair, downcast and dismayed. We hardly know what to say or what to do.

It was an awful night. She doesn't know anything about the situation of her husband or the other Belgians.

Sunday, November 29

A fairly calm night. Will they come today and get us also? The mood around here is not the best. We do not go to the High Mass, and we cannot eat at the mission.

At nine o'clock: Jean de Strooper is suddenly brought back. He looks tired, but otherwise he's fine. We gather around him, curious for some news. He says that he cannot say anything, except that we, the fathers and brothers, shouldn't be afraid.

Mr. Godin is at the hospital.

Brother Lambert announces that all the Simba are going to march on Buta.

A calm evening.

We don't know anything more and we are waiting for something to happen.

Monday, November 30

Tonight: About three o'clock, some shooting. In the morning we learn that the series of executions has begun again, including, among others, some officers who were preparing their "retreat."

Five o'clock in the afternoon: Titule has been taken. Forty whites have been liberated. Our opinion: this could go on for weeks.

Tuesday, December 1

At the mission, there's so much going on all the time. The

diocesan priests have moved out because of the "visitors" who believe that this is a hotel.

Five o'clock in the afternoon: The sisters arrive to distract us, Father Fons Kuypers and myself, with a card party. A moral problem: a European woman was raped several times last week. Now she's afraid that she is pregnant and wants to have an abortion. We can't do anything. One of the kinder Simba saved her and brought her to the sisters'. She can't say anything, but it's well understood that she didn't have one peaceful night. Hideous. We decide to keep everything quiet.

Wednesday, December 2

About half of us celebrate Mass and the other half go to communion. Advent has begun, and certain texts of the Mass and the Breviary seem more directly addressed to us than ever before.

The summer is beautiful, refreshing. A real dry season.

Five o'clock in the afternoon: At the mission, everything has been moved. Brother Leo has also received some money for his work at the garage.

They say that we're departing for Buta.

A little later, a black brother brings us the news that Bunia has been taken but that they couldn't find one single white person. Some other news about Bondo comes to us in the meantime: a young girl from the Norwegian Protestant Mission was kidnapped by Augustine in person. He rode all around with her in the car and asked that she marry him. Naturally, she refused, and it seems, a little afterward, he let her go peacefully.

He also wanted to take some of the African sisters, but they were able to get rid of him thanks to a little money.

Thursday, December 3

Opening of the Eucharistic Congress at Bombay. The pope will be there.

In the morning: Good news arrives during breakfast: Ango has been taken. The first Crosiers have been liberated…And when will our turn be? Father Frans Waldram has been confined to his room for some days: he has jaundice. One of the Capuchin fathers has also

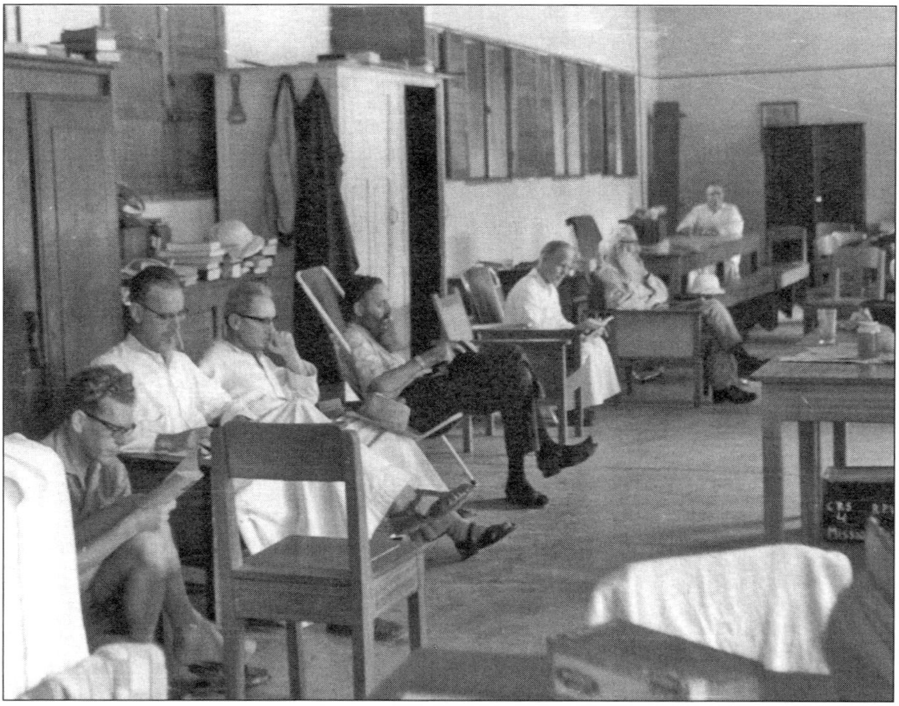

Above: Reading "wallflowers" are dispersed throughout the room (December 9, 1964). Below: the sisters gather together. *(Photos courtesy of the Crosier Province of Blessed Theodore de Celles, Europe.)*

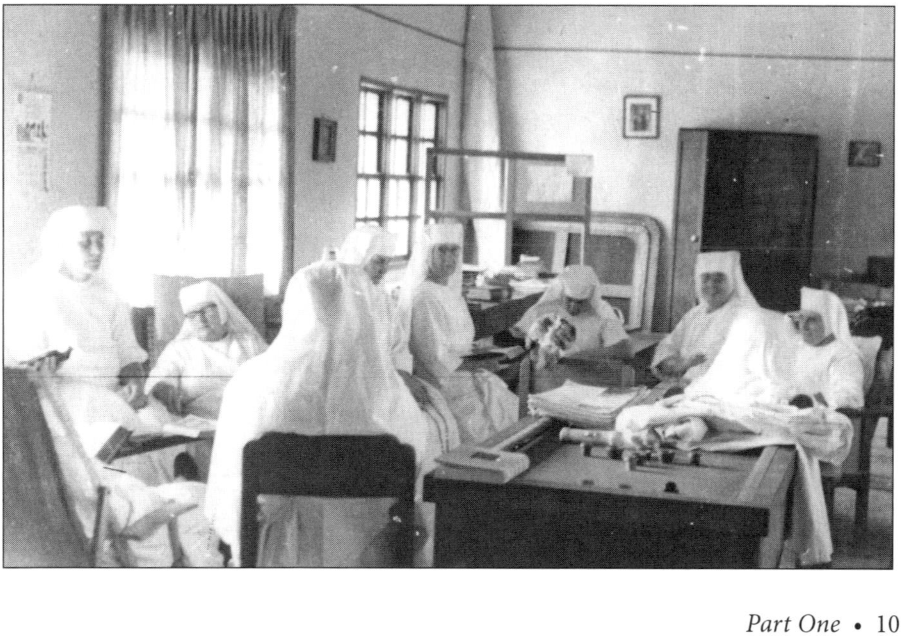

been sick for some days.

Friday, December 4

After dinner, during the siesta, we hear a truck approaching, accompanied by a lot of noise and cries. We wake up and get into our clothes, ready for the worst. We go out, but it's for nothing. Some bawling Simba come for a battery. We notice that we have become hyper-sensitive.

In the evening, while we were going to sleep, two diocesan priests come to announce that Father Richard who was still at Ndukula was badly harassed by a group of Simba. They stole from him; he has arrived in Bondo and is now hiding in a house.

We also learn that during the past week, four Simba who were going to flee were slain under the flag, while four members of RADECO were thrown into the Uele after their legs had been broken.

Saturday, December 5

It seems that Father Richard will be released today. They beat him up again and stole everything he had.

In the evening: It's not without some bittersweet humor that one thinks this evening of Saint Nicholas' Day at home.

Sunday, December 6

Yesterday, late in the evening, we had another "surprise": the loud visit of two drunk chiefs: lieutenants Vincent and Andre. They came simply to inspect things…

According to the news, it seems that today the "retaking" of Buta will become a reality. The day before, fourteen truckloads of soldiers had departed for Paulis.

For the rest, it's a peaceful Sunday.

At six thirty: It's dusk outside. Someone pulls my attention to a beautiful scene: two of the fathers are outside praying their rosary. They pray, most probably, for a rapid and prosperous peace. Two of our guards are also running a rosary through their hands, as Father Snijkers says. Only their intentions probably don't accord with those of the fathers. "They are praying to advance their own interests," sighs someone at my side who then disappears behind his book.

During evening recreation: Father Jan van Wagenberg plays billiards. One of our guards watches him; he wears his sunglasses (though we have excellent fluorescent lights), with his helmet on his head and revolver in his hand.

Monday, December 7

A peaceful day. The sisters, who come often to give shots to the sick here, say that the Simba are occupied in looting the house of a white who is in prison.

Tuesday, December 8

After the Conventual Mass, competition at a checker game serves as a stimulant.

Niangara has fallen now. The Dominicans were led out.

Wednesday, December 9

Monotony has taken hold of us. There's nothing that goes on. For about the last month now, this is the way we "use" our time: the first ones get up around six o'clock. The ambiance is like a summer camp; people wash with their shirts off at the long row of seminarians' sinks. Most of us go to chapel until about seven thirty, while our layman, de Strooper, cleans up our hall. Then, Brother Lambert brings the coffee and the news. With our bread, some cheese! And it's been like that for months. There must be a lot of stock on hand.

After the meal (during which we hash over again, yes, the political situation), we do the dishes, make our beds, and prepare ourselves slowly for the Conventual Mass.

Afterward, the games begin: billiards, cards, Scrabble, checkers, and chess. Everywhere in the hall, there are those who sit and read alongside the long walls. A regular delivery of new reading material is necessary; we devour a lot; everywhere the tables are covered with Catholic periodicals and digests of various sorts, etc. And so we pass the mornings. There are days when the time passes more quickly and agreeably. If one wants, in the meantime, one can go take a shower or visit one's room, provided one has permission. Most of our guards are friendly, and they are happy to eat at our table. We eat at twelve thirty and then take a siesta. Most of us go to the dormitory, but some stretch out in a chair in the recreation room on one chair or two. We wake up about three o'clock. These months fortunately there are tons of oranges, lemons, and bananas, so immediately after sleeping we can have a refreshing dessert. As far as the freshness goes, we thank the one who had the good idea to bring along our refrigerator.

One must be peaceful until three thirty. We pray and read a little. Then, there's coffee and often a volleyball match. Supper is at seven thirty and to bed at ten o'clock. Often it's very pleasant in the obscurity of the dormitory, just before we fall asleep, despite the mosquitoes, which are often pestiferous.

Thursday, December 10

Following the news that the army of liberation has marched from Stanleyville to Buta, we live with a new hope.

There is never any news about the whites imprisoned in Bondo. Are they still alive?

Very early in the morning, some Simba from Baye come to see the pastor, (Father Gerard) Kester. In a ditch they found some hidden rifles. They ask if he knew something about them.

In the evening: Hearing that one of their confreres had been killed there, the fathers of Yakoma are very downcast. We don't believe but half of everything, but even so one is never tranquil.

Another communication: Paulis has fallen.

Friday, December 11

In fifteen days, it will be Christmas. Will we be home? We still have a hope.

At noon, Vincent comes to tell us that we should walk around more. To be all the time locked up is not good for your health, he says. We don't ask for anything better of ourselves, but continue our life of being at camp. In a little while, perhaps a new chief will impose new and more severe restrictions on us.

Two letters from Monsignor Creemers circulate among us after the volleyball match. They come from Bangassou thanks to an Arab. It seems that the Monsignor doesn't know anything. He even wants to come here. In the meantime, he will indeed learn a little more.

Saturday, December 12

No news. A terribly unnerving Saturday.

Sunday, December 13

In the morning, the Simba communicate that Augustine has now re-conquered Aketi (but of course there are reservations about news coming from such a source.)

And, if it's true...

In the evening, they bring back Father Vissers with so much noise that our hearts stop. All ends well.

This evening also, I learn, by chance, that three whites at Bondo were assassinated fifteen days ago. We knew all three. We don't speak any more.[25]

Monday, December 14

Another unnerving day.

Tuesday, December 15

De Strooper is invited to a party the Simba are having.

Wednesday, December 16

This morning, the Golden Mass.[26] We are no longer thinking that we will be liberated by Christmas.

Communications on the radio: Cardinal Suenens has received in audience one hundred missionaries from the Congo. The first missionaries are coming back in a little while...

Thursday, December 17

Have they really forgotten about us? Each of us hopes yet to be home for Christmas, even though the chances are getting slimmer by the day.

---

25 Misters Hourt, Lempereur, and Raymond Legros. During the night of November 28 and 29, with their hands and feet tied behind their backs, they were thrown into the Uele. But Legros was able to free himself and reach the shore by swimming. He hid himself at Bondo until the liberation by the South African mercenaries on May 26, 1965.

26 Before Vatican II, just before Christmas, when the Gospel of the Annunciation was read, sometimes golden vestments were used.

Friday, December 18

A Portuguese is heard on the radio who says that there are still 160 whites who are awaiting their liberation in Bondo. The number is a little elevated, but they haven't forgotten us.

In the afternoon, the adjutant Paul comes to say that some fathers will pass the feasts of Christmas with the people at Monga and Baye.

It seems that Aketi has indeed again been taken by the rebels: today in Bondo they are getting together some groups of men to go down there.

PART TWO

Deported to Buta

Saturday, December 19

Just before the Conventual Mass, some soldiers come to announce to us that we must depart immediately to...Buta. We just have enough time to throw together some things, like a blanket and a pillow. In the disorder of the moment, some watches are requisitioned in a brutal tone of voice. We catch on right away to what is going on, and after the first victims, nobody else seems to have a watch.

Then a rapid departure. This is not going rapidly enough for the rebels, who are grouped around the truck, rifle on the shoulder and a blasting radio in hand.

They go also to get the Brothers of Saint Gabriel. They want to take along the sisters, too, but it's impossible because now the truck is full to overflowing: some of us are happy to have a place... standing. We ride on over to the sisters', who are all ready to go and equipped from head to toe (they were apparently already aware of this yesterday evening), but after some discussion, they have to wait for another truck.

All of the diocesan priests are around the truck when we depart a little later. The mood is not a very happy one.

They take us to the prison, where we have to get off and enter. In the shadows of the courtyard we wait for what will happen. In our opinion, Buta is still in the hands of the National Congolese Army. We are there, to wait, and nobody knows what we are waiting for. It goes on like this for an hour and a half.

We get back on the truck then and pass over the Uele in the ferryboat and set out in the direction of Buta. The driver is driving fast. The sisters and a whole group of whites are waiting for us at Likati. They are going to accompany us, but that seems impossible: they are able to go back home and wait for a truck that will transport the sisters from Bondo.

After a stop of one and one-half hours, we roll at high speed

Some of the hostages at Buta spend some time outdoors. *(Photo courtesy of the Crosier Province of Blessed Theodore de Celles, Europe.)*

in the direction of Buta. Along the route, we cannot eat anything or hardly drink anything.

When we get to Buta, it is in the dark of night. We are immediately taken to the sisters' mission, where the bishop of Buta, Monsignor Jacques Mbali, cordially welcomes us, as does Augustine (who has been named a colonel) a few minutes later. The black sisters come all around the truck, that is, a group of them, for about thirty sisters have not yet been found since their flight from Buta at the arrival of the rebels.

The colonel is very friendly. He says that we will be lodged in the house of the Marist Brothers. The Simba who are lodging there now must leave this evening. We will eat a bit first at the mission of the Premonstratensians. At the table, unbelievable stories make the round: the bishop had asked Augustine to transport the sisters and the fathers from Bondo to Buta in order to permit them to leave from here to Europe. We hear again the horrible stories of the pillaging organized here by two armies and under the unmentionable conduct of the mercenaries. The National Congolese Army had, for example, slain wounded Simba right where they lay, lodged here at the hospital with no chance of getting away. They even carted away from the hospital everything possible and then destroyed the rest.

After the very sober meal, a group of us makes our way to the house of the Marist Brothers, where things are rather "unsettled." The Simba do not want to leave. There is an exchange of words. The house is also in a pitiable state: it was looted twice. Even the mercenaries lodged here, and I found the passport of one of them in my room. We go to bed. But it is hardly a question of sleeping. In the middle of the night, they come again to make an inspection of the rooms. They bark and get angry for one reason or another.

Sunday, December 20

Our group (those who had lodged at the Marist Brothers) goes to Mass with a large escort. Among ourselves we mumble: if only we had been allowed to stay at Bondo where it was certainly more pleasant. After breakfast at the mission of the Premonstratensians, we are obliged to go to the recreation room at the Marists' house, and a little after that, Colonel Augustine comes to announce that there will be an inspection of the house.

We quickly notice that this is a very special inspection: everything is directly destroyed. This is the third time that they are "working over" the house in this manner. And I have to say that this both hurts and makes one want to swear; on the other hand, it's laughable, but it still hits you. Our troop of "little chicks" hears and sees everything. It's very disgusting. And it goes on for hours. Some of us say among ourselves: we see now why we had to leave Bondo; they are going to do the same thing there.

Toward four o'clock in the afternoon (we had a little to eat about noon but with no appetite), the ambiance does a flip-flop. They dance (they are content with the booty: clothes, musical instruments, etc.), they come over to us to shake our hands, they are now again friendly. The commander comes to make a speech; he speaks of the fact of their having weapons as if he were a prophet; and then comes the real high point of the evening—he exposes his bruised rear end…From then on we can sleep where we want to (we all naturally go to the mission).

In the evening: We all go to retire at the mission of the fathers. We eat a little, for there isn't much. That's becoming a problem here. We didn't bring anything, and there are very few provisions here. We all look for a place to sleep at the mission; some of us are four in a room.

Monday, December 21

It was peaceful all day. There are no guards. We are all now at the mission, and here we stay. There's hardly anything to smoke anymore. Too bad that we had to leave Bondo in such haste.

The bishop comes to see us (he always stays at the sisters') and told us the story of the liberation of Buta and how the National Congolese Army set up here. It seems that we are obliged to change our idealized conceptions of the National Congolese Army.

We also learn why the Simba were so angry yesterday when they looted the house of the Marists. One of the black Marist Brothers who was here had, for a long time, wanted to get rid of the Simba, and for that reason had written some letters to the colonel, which were intercepted by the Simba. That enraged them, and they demanded his

From left: Fons Kuypers, osc; Monulf Schrijvers, ofm cap.; Adriaan van den Broucke, ofm cap.; Jan Verhoeven, osc; Huub van Lieshout, osc; Guido de Zwaef, Brother of Saint Gabriel; Leo Ignoul, osc; Albert Timmers, osc; and Rob Carremans, osc. (Photo courtesy of the Crosier Province of Blessed Theodore de Celles, Europe.)

death. During that time, the brother was thrust into prison and was only liberated thanks to the supplications of the black sisters (who are obliged to take care of all the colonel's chores, for he has a weak side for them).

The bishop still hopes that soon we will be taken to neutral terrain where we can then move on to freedom.

In the evening: Father Jan van Wagenberg is suddenly seized with a malaise, a little attack we think. Brother Bernard de Kegel suffers from kidney stones.

Tuesday, December 22

It is peaceful before noon. The sisters of Bondo and the Canonesses of the Holy Sepulcher from Likati arrive before dinner. Some Protestant pastors, and Mrs. Legros and her two children, accompany them. The sister superior gives us a report of the trip.

Wednesday, December 23

A truck will leave today for Bondo to get some food and other things that seem indispensable. Father Vissers and Brothers Lambert and Leo will be going.

Thursday, December 24

It seems that Father Godefrooy should be going to Baye on Monday in order to print some papers for the Simba. There are always some of us who are ill. Happily, the sisters are here now. In company with the white and the black sisters we practice the chants for the Christmas liturgy. By order of the colonel, there will be a Solemn Mass at midnight tonight.

Around eleven thirty, Brother Leo returns from Bondo with some soldiers. He recounts for us how the soldiers had killed during the trip, on the side of the road, a captain who was refusing to obey their orders (it was a question of using a telephone). At the end, Leo had to take the wheel, since the Simba chauffeur had drunk too much.

Then, we went to Mass at midnight. There was not a mouse in the church, except for about twenty soldiers armed to their teeth and Colonel Augustine, who, dressed in civilian clothes, sat in a special chair up front. The three Masses began. All the fathers, brothers, and sisters are in the choir and sing well. At the moment when we sing the introit chant[27], despite the situation, we enter into the Christmas mood.

During the consecration, something particularly frightening happened. We did see some soldiers go out, and then we heard the cocking of the rifles set to fire, and then during the silence of the consecration, the machine guns began to sputter at the door with an incredible noise. Unconsciously, we bent over. Noise enough to announce the end of the world.

A little later, during the distribution of Holy Communion, we sang "Silent Night, Holy Night." After Mass, we wished each other a "Merry Christmas" while drinking a glass of cold water, and we spoke a little about how sensational it was.

Friday, December 25

At nine o'clock we celebrated the Solemn High Mass, this time, fortunately, without the military salutes. At noon, a black brother brought us a bottle of Cinzano and two bottles of Ricard. Delicious! We haven't seen any strong drinks for at least two months. We're saving a little for the New Year.

Saturday, December 26

The second day of Christmas. There are numerous shots fired during the course of the morning, but here they leave us in peace. We can walk around freely, even outside of the house, but we stay inside for the most part.

In the evening: We have a fearful moment—a truck loaded with singing soldiers stops in front. We go to see what's going on, but these are our brave men: Father Vissers and Brother Lambert are there along with many Simba and lots of food and other things for us from Bondo. Everybody quickly helps to unload the cases, boxes, and packages. Everybody is in a good mood. Even the Simba. Again we have some wine for Mass, coffee, powdered milk, butter, flour, and something to smoke. They did very well for the trip. Everything was peaceful in Bondo. There has been some burglary already at the

27 Entrance antiphon

seminary but so far nothing serious. We aren't making any guesses about the future.

Sunday, December 27

A fair amount of people are at Mass. The people begin to reappear; without a doubt, our presence here gives them some security. Many people go to confession. In the meantime we learn that many of the head rebels from Bondo, Likati, and other places are being called here. Without a doubt, they are preparing something.

Monday, December 28

The Feast of the Holy Innocents. A day to wash clothes. When I go over to the sisters' to get some laundry detergent, I see, for the first time this year, a Nativity scene.

A black brother from Aketi arrives before dinner. He had accompanied some white fathers, but he returned soon after. Aketi is now for the second time under the regime of the rebels. In fact, they occupy the town. This is important for them for getting gasoline. They are not yet at Bumba.

The bishop of Lolo (whom we had encountered before at Stanleyville) is at Bumba. A courageous man. The mission of Aketi has been completely looted.

Tuesday, December 29

Our neighbors, the Simba, have become more and more irritating. They are again living in the mission house of the Marists. One could say that their manner of irritating us is…musical. They have taken over the trumpets and other horns, but they are far from being good musicians. They came and asked Brother Gilbert Asselman to be their musical director, and it was difficult for him to refuse.

In the evening: Radio Leopoldville announces that an airplane will come to reconnoiter Buta tomorrow. We are as afraid of planes as we are of the Simba.

Wednesday, December 30

The sisters say that eleven people have been killed here today in Buta, among them were the directors of the women nationalists. The president of the party was also among the victims. It seems that everything revolves around who's controlling the money. An uneasy evening: a lot of shooting.

Thursday, December 31

We are going to make up a liturgical calendar for next year. Again a lot of shooting today. We're getting used to it. This evening, Saint Sylvester's Party.

Friday, January 1

New Year's Day. We sing the High Mass at the sisters'.

At noon: There's still something "hidden behind the wood pile" for a pre-dinner drink. Augustine, who comes often to eat and to converse at the sisters', says that the administrator of Bondo has asked for the return of the sisters to take care of the sick, the wounded, and the pregnant women. So, a few sisters could return, although the superior says that they will postpone the departure as long as possible.

The bishop (who comes regularly to our house) says that Augustine told him that he wants to flee. Today he asked the black sisters what they would like for a gift for the New Year. They asked him to forbid the soldiers to be shooting all day. He granted their request.

Saturday, January 2

We are talking more and more about an eventual return to Bondo. Now that Christmas and New Year's have passed, we are not hoping to be liberated soon, and we'd rather be at work at Bondo.

Sunday, January 3

There are more and more people at church. Colonel Augustine was there today too. Since the incident at the brothers' house, he comes only rarely to see us. It was different at Bondo.

Monday, January 4

Today, there was going to be a solemn service for a major who was killed at Aketi. But it turned out much differently. At eight o'clock, we heard the first shots. It was violent and it went on and on. And then there was a pause, and then it began again even more violently and there was a response. The heaviest artillery was now being used. We all went back to our house. There was more and more shooting. Then, all of a sudden, we saw the first soldiers on the road taking flight. Their panic was easy to see. A few cars passed. A fantastic sensation took hold of us: the National Congolese Army was attacking Buta, and in a few hours, we would be FREE!

The shooting died down a little later. There was a crisp silence. We didn't see anybody on the road.

After another half-hour, we had the whole story. Augustine has since confirmed it. He had left early in the morning and had simulated an attack. Only a few officers and some of the black sisters knew what was happening. Today was the payment of salaries. Only those who didn't take flight will be paid, which means a nice stack of money is left over for the colonel.

In the evening: To have something to do, we go to harvest some coffee.

Tuesday, January 5

In the evening: Two diocesan priests were brought here from Aketi. The bishop had asked them to come. Everything is destroyed at Aketi. They say that the fathers and the whites have had to endure a lot during the last days before the liberation. That was due especially to a captain who is still alive and at times is seen here at Buta. There will be some differences between him and Augustine.

Wednesday, January 6

Feast of the Kings. There are many black kings but not enough wise men…

Thursday, January 7

At quarter to noon, "Crazy Paul," whom we had known before at Bondo, comes to greet us. He is, as usual, very friendly and tolerably drunk. One wonders if these guys don't become a little crazy after a while. One notices, among certain ones, that their continual drinking

From left: Hendrik Verberk, osc; Marinus Godefrooy, osc; Leo Ignoul, osc; and Guido de Zwaef, Brother of Saint Gabriel. *(Photo courtesy of the Crosier Province of Blessed Theodore de Celles, Europe.)*

Missionaries in Buta—Standing (from left to right): Willem Vissers, osc; Marcel Smits, osc; Lambert Schoenmakers, osc; Bernard De Kegel, Brother of Saint Gabriel; Guido de Zwaef, Brother of Saint Gabriel; Laurent Bosmans, Brother of Saint Gabriel; Willem Tieken, osc; Marinus Godefrooy, osc; and Filip Waldram, osc. Kneeling (from left to right): Hendrik Verberk, osc; Adriaan van den Broucke, ofm cap.; Rik Snijkers, osc; Jef Beckers, osc; and Leo Ignoul, osc.
(Photo courtesy of the Crosier Province of Blessed Theodore de Celles, Europe.)

leads to the use of marijuana, and finally exhausts them and leaves them in a stupefied state.

Friday, January 8

The colonel comes back again to ask for some "Belga" cigarettes. There are no more. Neither is there tobacco for a pipe. They don't say anything, but some of the older ones are beginning to feel the lack of something. In considering all, we were able to smoke for quite a long time. There was a great reserve at Bondo, and we had a lot of "Albert" cigarettes when we were on our trip to Stanleyville.

Saturday, January 9

They are really leaving us in peace here. It's extraordinary. From that point of view, it's better here at Buta than at Bondo.

Sunday, January 10

We are beginning to swim regularly in the Rubi, a river that flows behind the mission. It's an ideal relaxation for men who are always locked up.

Monday, January 11

Last night, they killed four people again, one of whom was a captain who was found responsible for embezzling four million francs.

The sisters are saying that this captain, after floating four hours in the water, came back. He was not dead but wounded. He says that he was even in paradise and that, while there, they told him there would be an attack against Dinglia on January 15.

Tuesday, January 12

The mood among us is getting better and better. The sick ones are getting better. We eat well. The swimming is good for many of us. We have found a pile of skirts for young girls in a room, and we transform them into swim suits. In another room, we found a treasure of novels.

A soldier comes to tell us that the population has cut down some trees on the road to Dinglia and that that should stop the attack; is this true?

After dinner: We learn that there's a big chance that we will all be able to return to Bondo.

Wednesday, January 13

Before dinner, we learn that only the fathers will return to Bondo. (A lot of news comes to us from the black sisters, who transmit it to us through the white sisters.) Most of us prefer to stay here.

In the evening, Paul, who is drunk, comes to tell us that five soldiers of the National Congolese Army are in Buta. For the time being, they will not be shot. This is in light of a cease-fire.

Thursday, January 14

We are very surprised when we learn that de Strooper is leaving today to go to Banalia to repair the road, the ferryboat, etc. This was bombed by the others. The colonel says that there is no danger because the Simba are in control there and that they are already about ten miles from Stanleyville...Again our illusions evaporate. In the meantime, the sisters are hard at work on a beautiful dress for a certain "Mama Maria," a mother-of-the-troops, who should obtain for them some "dawa" (magic medicine) tomorrow before they depart for combat.

Radio Leopoldville denies again that Stanleyville would soon be again in the hands of the Simba.

Friday, January 15

In the morning, Brother Peerke comes back from the sisters with some bread and some funny news. That woman for whom the sisters were making the beautiful dress was not a mother-of-the-troops, but simply a devious woman, who wanted a dress to be finished as soon as possible and who had invented the rest.

In mid-morning: Father Jan van Wagenberg makes up a list of those who would like to return to Bondo. We would like to make a proposition, by the mediation of the bishop: a large part of our group would return to Bondo because of the lack of food here, whereas the sick would remain, not far from the sisters.

For the rest, we are doing well here. The ambiance is not bad.

Our only hope—beyond that of liberation—is that they might know at home in Europe that we are well here.

In the evening: The sisters bring us some big news: the colonel was at the sisters at four o'clock, and he had to leave immediately for Aketi, for the others were attacking in force. The tension mounts again in us.

Saturday, January 16

Yesterday evening, the colonel came to our place again for a moment. It seemed like a "good-bye" in connection with the attack at Aketi. Today, we don't hear anything more.

Tuesday, January 19

These last days, no news. Long boring days. All of the communications that could give us hope are immediately dashed. The needle on "our" barometer swings from one side to the other... tired. The return to Bondo is put into question because of the events at Aketi.

Wednesday, January 20

In the morning: A letter from the diocesan priests in Bondo arrives. Peace reigns there, and after a first small looting episode, there was not a second; that makes us happy. Everything is calm here also. The National Congolese Army had, in fact, launched an attack against Aketi a few days ago, but was pushed back.

What we think now is: this could go on for months.

Quarter after twelve: Radio Brussels announces that Bondo has been taken and is liberated. About twenty whites were liberated. We all are talking about this sensational news in the dining room. So much so that the soup got cold. It is almost impossible to believe. If it is true, again, we've had fabulously bad luck!

During the day, we keep our eyes on the Simba. But they are hiding their feelings well.

After tea: They bury one of their big shots. The great improvised fanfare is something for fairy tales. The military salute with rifle is on the same par with the music...

In the evening: Colonel Augustine brings a package of letters that was waiting for months at Bangassou. We are very happy. There is lots of old news, but for us it is new. Augustine promises us more mail. It is very friendly of him.

Thursday, January 21

Augustine gave the sisters time "off" so that they can write some letters for Europe. The letters will leave soon for Bangassou by way of Bondo. So, Bondo is always in their hands…

Friday, January 22

In the morning: We drank some cocoa to celebrate the forty years of marriage of the parents of Father Frans Waldram. We are preparing some mail for Bangassou.

In the evening: We learn that the mail will be delayed. The colonel is angry, and we cannot send anything. Is there something true then about the subject of Bondo?

Saturday, January 23

A truck full of Arabs left this morning for Bondo in order to look for some other instruments for parades, etc. The role of the Arabs is fairly dubious in this revolution. We are almost certain that they pass on regularly some munitions by way of Bangassou.

Yesterday: Augustine solemnly promised, yet another time, to protect all the sisters and the fathers and the brothers, even if it means his death.

Sunday, January 24

A fair amount of people in church. After the High Mass, we have again some fairly pleasant discussions in front of the church about more peaceful times. And to give it all some more animation, after the High Mass, Augustine chases around with the black sisters on a jeep taken from the enemy (complete with a mounted machine gun). The sisters know how to play this game well.

Monday, January 25

The sisters tell us how Augustine, in playing cards with the religious superior (which they were doing fairly regularly already in Bondo), spoke again of the letters that we were not able to write. They rapidly put together a telegram that they confided to him. It was authorized.

The rumor is making the rounds among the Simba that there will be a forceful attack mounted against Buta at the end of this week.

Tuesday, January 26

A dull day. No news. We're awaiting the return of the truck that departed for Bondo.

Wednesday, January 27

During the night: We were awakened by a truck that stopped here in front of the mission. The diocesan priest Father Marcel of Likati was inside with others. He informed us that there was nothing that happened in Bondo. Radio Brussels had nevertheless broadcast the news twice. This communication should have made a lot of noise in Europe.

Thursday, January 28

During the morning we were occupied in trying to play "bridge" when some military maneuvers around the mission became too real. The head coverings of 150 well-armed Simba are something to notice: a kind of Arab head covering. The colonel directed the maneuvers about which we had been warned in advance.

Friday, January 29

There are more and more swimmers…Even the Simba and their "ladies" are in line to get in; they swim or wash their clothes.

The colonel (it seems that the Simba call him "Cornelius") comes to recreation in the evening to talk about a tape deck that isn't working. He is, as usual, dressed with distinction.

Sunday, January 31

The wounded are arriving from Aketi and the surrounding areas. There are two groups of them. So, there's something going on.

In the evening: By chance I hear something very interesting. When the black sisters, profiting from an opportune moment, ask

Augustine why the fathers and sisters are being so harassed, and if all this was necessary, the response was: Lumumba has established a plan of three phases. The first: The whites in the administration. That happened in '60. The second: Get rid of all the intellectuals who, in one fashion or another, do not belong to the party. That's what's going on now. The third phase: To nationalize the religion and to extradite the fathers who do not cooperate. A lot of the difficulties that the fathers have had up until now are due to the fact that some Simba believe that we have already entered into the third phase of the plan.

Tuesday, February 2

The news received these last days on the subject of Aketi is more complete. The Simba were in fact beaten again. There was also a horrible accident with a truck full of Simba. Many of the wounded have arrived here.

It's said that the Protestants, who have been brought here (for example the Reverend Paul), can now leave with their families for Bangassou. The "miss" is seriously ill.

The sisters learn from a Simba that, at Bondo, the diocesan priest Father Jean-Pierre is under a lot of tension and will be transported to Bangassou. It seems that there is a good chance that Mrs. Legros can also leave for Bangassou.

Wednesday, February 3

A peaceful day until about five thirty in the afternoon. We went through a particularly spectacular burial of a high officer who was recently killed at Aketi. He had been "formed" in Prague and Moscow. The burial ended with several mortar shots. The dust fell all over the place, even here, so heavy was the atmosphere. Fortunately, we had been warned ahead.

In the evening: Some more sensational news: it seems that the colonel had spoken at the black sisters' house of the eventual departure for Europe of the white sisters. They could leave on vacation for two months. The Reverend Paul came to visit us today. He's gotten skinny. He says not to believe much in the promises of the colonel, considering that he hasn't yet departed for Bangassou.

Thursday, February 4

Sister Jeanne, of Bondo, arrived here yesterday. She came to pay us a visit this morning. Everything is peaceful at Bondo, everything goes well, except that the diocesan priest Father Richard is very tense. The Simba, who had already brought this news to the sisters, made a mistake on the name. It's not Jean-Pierre but Richard.

Today, we organized our second bridge drive. There are always more swimmers.

We notice these days that there are always more and more Simba at Buta. That means that there will be an attack in force against Stanleyville.

Saturday, February 6

Charles, the captain at Bondo, has arrived here. He comes to see us and brings some letters. Some news! Among other things, we learn that the father of Brother Guido de Zwaef has died. The diocesan priests and the black brothers have escorted Father Richard to Bangassou. From there, he will continue to Bangui and perhaps even arrive in Europe. There's more news in the letters. The fathers at Bangassou have prepared some things to send us, food and other necessities, but they don't know how to get them to us. They don't know yet that we are at Buta. Here, food is becoming a problem again. We are eating dried-out bread all the time; the cheese (the eternal cheese of Bondo) is finished, the jam also.

After dinner, we have a visit from Jean de Strooper who came back from Banalia. He constructed a new ferryboat. There were many victims who fell during the day of the fall of Stanleyville, among them fathers and sisters and other whites. Everything is destroyed. Jean de Strooper made the acquaintance of another colonel there— a genial type, he says. He ardently desired an armistice. There are several thousand Simba who have assembled around Stanleyville to attack in force. According to the letters from the sisters and the brothers of Bondo, we have the impression that they are waiting for a liberation that is fairly close. They make us to understand, by disguised words, that they know more than that, and that this will not last very much longer.

Sunday, February 7

Today, there is a great celebration for the "lions" (Simba). The lieutenant-colonel Augustine is promoted to the rank of full colonel. After dinner, the orchestra offers a serenade at the sisters' house, where a big banquet has been organized.

Monday, February 8

After the Mass for the father of Brother Guido de Zwaef, our Monday washing of clothes is interrupted by an important visit that is announced to us by Bishop Jacques. One of the high civil authorities is coming to pay us a visit. Augustine accompanies him. He has a friendly appearance. He gives a short speech in perfect French. Its contents: the time of murders has passed. We shouldn't think of that and regret anything…We absolutely should not be afraid. Our security is guaranteed. He has come to visit us to ask for two fathers who would go to Banalia and two others to Bengamissa. Some lower echelon officers will be formed there (at Bengamissa) and, if we accept to collaborate with them, they will particularly appreciate it. The others who want to go back home can depart.

Since we had no idea of how to respond to all of this, they took leave and left us in a particularly strange mood.

During dinner: Brothers Leo and Marcel left for Bondo in order to look for a motor for a jeep. It's rainy today. The laundry will have to wait until the sun comes out tomorrow.

In the evening: The sisters tell us that they had the same visit as we did; the black sisters did as well. Everywhere, they demanded a sharing of the personnel. All the sisters are afraid of this proposal. The black sisters are particularly afraid. Augustine, on several occasions, has let it be understood that he would separate the sisters and give them to his officers…Since the visit of this person, the sisters are taking turns going two by two to chapel to pray that none of this comes about. They ask us also to participate, and a list is drawn up.

In the afternoon: The colonel finds the black sisters "down in the dumps." He asks them if they were so down because of this visit. They don't say much. Then he cries out: "And if **I** didn't want it, now…"

Tuesday, February 9

In the morning: Captain Vincent comes here to have a radio repaired (Father Kraewinkels never had so much work; everybody has a radio and nobody knows anything about them). He tells us that all the fathers and all the sisters, those who are at Bili also, have to come to Stanleyville after the fall of that city. We will be among the first members of the new free state, and, as such, we will be treated as valuable material…

After dinner: Two trucks full of soldiers leave for Aketi. The shooting is intense today.

Wednesday, February 10

After dinner: The brothers come back from Bondo with the jeep motor and a lot of news. First of all is the news that our Dutch confreres Nol (Arnold) Vervoort and Wim (Willem) van Wetten and also a sister from England were assassinated at Dakwa during the bloody days of the fall of Stanleyville. We broke down at the news.[28] The brothers were also able to explain two communiqués announcing a rapid liberation. The diocesan priests encountered at Bangassou a Greek of Buta, Cristo, who is engaged as a mercenary. He was saying that they will be departing from Yakoma soon to "work" quickly in using as much force as possible. He recounted also that the soldiers of the National Congolese Army had received an order not to kill Augustine or Charles, because they had protected the missionaries.

There is another confused communiqué: a grade-school teacher from Bili has told us that, at Bili, where one of our brothers is working with three sisters, some vehicles arrived one day and that they transported away all the personnel of the mission except one diocesan priest.

But what army did this?

After dinner: We learn that the people in question at Bili are at Titule. According to the colonel, Sister Paula will soon be able to leave on vacation.

---

28 The two fathers were assassinated November 25, along with Sister Margaret Bradley, an English Ursuline, and a Portuguese merchant of Dakwa, Mr. Nunes. These murders, along with many others, were part of the revenge for the taking of Stanleyville by the mercenaries and the National Congolese Army.

Friday, February 12

Today, some negotiations begin at Nairobi. We are hoping for a kind of solution. Yesterday evening, Sister Paula said to the colonel: "You are lying to me." He spontaneously reacted: "On Friday, you will receive your papers for departure, and you will leave on Saturday."

In the meantime, we learn more on the subject of the "murder-party" of Banalia and that area. Incredible. We had seen these people when we were on our trip to Stanleyville.

Yesterday, a truck arrived from Bondo with some things for us. The smokers are especially happy about this.

Saturday, February 13

Sister Paula still doesn't have her papers. The black sisters think that it's because of the tension in the air since yesterday, when there arrived some wounded from Aketi. It seems that some planes intervened down there.

The black sisters told us a funny one. It's thanks to them that we have obtained some favors from the colonel. A few days ago, they were praying at the grotto of the Blessed Virgin. Augustine arrived in his Mercedes and tooted his horn. They did not lift up their heads, but continued praying. He came up behind them slowly. One of them said to him finally, "Kneel down and pray a little." That he did, but he added very quickly, "Not too long, for I don't know how to pray well when I am in uniform..."

The colonel has asked Sister Paula again for a little patience. They are fighting around Aketi. It seems that the conference at Nairobi can't get off the ground.

Sunday, February 14

A sunny Sunday morning. Augustine was at the High Mass. After Mass, he spoke with the bishop. A lot of soldiers are parading around or, rather, showing off. They are wearing some very good clothes, which they probably "found" here and there.

Monday, February 15

Some of us went down to the station to see what remained of

the trunks that had been sent to us. Everything was a big mess; all the boxes and trunks had been looted. They hold a sort of market here of things "found." Some suitcases of priestly vestments were given to us.

Tuesday, February 16

They are talking lately about a certain General Olenga, who will soon come to Buta with reinforcements.

In the evening: We learn from Radio Hilversum that, altogether, 126 missionaries have been killed, of which 11 were Dutch. There are others who are reported as "missing."

Wednesday, February 17

A lot of new guns have arrived. The soldiers are already carrying them around. The hospital sisters assisted this morning at a parade. They estimate that the number of Simba is around two thousand.

We are speaking again of our return to Bondo.

Friday, February 19

The colonel has made known to the Protestants that they should hold themselves ready to depart for Bangassou.

In the evening: Sister Paula comes to say good-bye. Two sisters, the Protestants, and Mrs. Legros and her two children can depart tomorrow morning. Could this be true?

Saturday, February 20

Sister Paula did not leave today, nor did the others. But the car that should've taken them did depart. We don't know anything about the Protestants. Perhaps only they departed?

Sunday, February 21

Yesterday, Augustine did not visit the sisters once during the day, which is exceptional. He had a lot of work to do to try to uncover a plot directed against him, which has now been discovered.

After the morning Mass: Another big piece of news: the colonel promised Brother Marcel Smits that he would depart on furlough with Sister Paula.

Monday, February 22

After Mass this morning, some other sudden news. Augustine spoke again of a departure yesterday evening while at the sisters'. What's more, besides the sisters, he spoke of the departure of Brother Marcel (he also spoke of Brother Leo Ignoul), and that two fathers could accompany them as far as Bangassou in order to purchase some necessities. Everything would be arranged for today (the car and the papers), and they would be able to depart tomorrow.

At noon: We learn that the Simba have set themselves up in the boarding school of the sisters.

After dinner: We learn that two sisters have received authorization for a sixty-day furlough. But again, nothing is arranged for the others.

Tuesday, February 23

They say that the departure should have taken place today. Fathers Frans Waldram and Willem Vissers will accompany the others in order to purchase some provisions.

In the evening: The "travelers" are still here. Over the radio we hear that there will be a great day of reparation in Rome and in Leopoldville in honor of all the victims of the Congo. The colonel has offered a pickup truck to Brother Venance.

Thursday, February 25

One doesn't hear anything of the departure for Bangassou. Days like this help us to understand just how much we are dependent on the Simba. At assembly this morning, Augustine made known these rules for the Simba:

They should not bother the peace of the fathers, sisters, and brothers; they cannot harass married women; and they should attend to their own food and pay for what they ask for. Those who don't obey will be severely punished.

Friday, February 26

A Protestant nurse[29] (of the English Baptist Church) arrived from Banalia yesterday and is now at the sisters'. She spoke the

29 Miss Margaret Hayes

whole evening. Some horrible things happened there. At a given moment, they started to assassinate all the whites (even a doctor who was operating on a Simba); she was warned and was able to flee into the woods. The Simba found her later and took her under their protection. She was taken to Buta by a general-major, who lost his rank and was arrested since he arrived…All this would be in connection with the mutiny against Augustine in which the Simba in and around Banalia were participating. It seems that more and more the organization is falling apart and that each group wants to be independent.

Augustine himself is at Zobia where there would later be some quarrels between the population and the Simba: this also makes us wonder.

Saturday, February 27

Most of us are suffering from diarrhea. The sisters have brought over some pills and powders. We can have some handkerchiefs made up at the sisters'; Mrs. Legros and that English miss are making them for us.

Monday, March 1

The colonel has come back to Buta. His arrival, yesterday evening, was noisily celebrated with a lot of shooting, while the sky was lit up with the bullets leaving a trail.

Here we see the typical mentality of the soldiers: it's two or three days since the bishop asked the Simba of our vicinity not to use the school desks for fire wood. What would be left when the schools would soon be opening their doors? "Bah" they said, "we won't go to school any more. And we will send our children to Moscow."

Even though you don't hear much talk anymore about assassinations, it seems that there still are regular executions decreed by the People's Court. People turn one another in. The Simba have discovered a new method: they wire up their victims and then turn on an electrical current. They do this on the bridge over the Rubi River in such a way that the bodies fall immediately into the water and are carried downstream.

One family starving to death arrived at Bengamissa. A small child died on the way, while a second is very weak at the hospital. The people suffer a lot during these days. And we only learn about half of it.

Tuesday, March 2, Carnival

At noon, the colonel brings some postcards from home written in French. They are even of a recent date: the beginning of February. There is a letter from the Reverend Paul that arrives from Bangassou. They are there for a long time already. Augustine was at the black sisters' house yesterday evening, and his chatter made the sisters again very pessimistic. It could be a question of a trick on his part, but here is what he recounted: a complaint had been brought up against Augustine to the general. He was occupying himself with politics, because of his contacts with the mission, and especially "with a group of young girls who live with no purpose in the convent at Buta." Because of this, Augustine has counseled the black sisters to throw away their garments and to return home. They are really very depressed at the moment.

In the evening: A black sister suddenly comes to tell us that Brother Marcel should leave immediately for Bangassou. One of the mechanics got some very corrosive acid in his eyes and they are going to try to transport him to Bangassou. Sisters Paula and Ida are to accompany them. Brother Marcel left hurriedly for the sisters'. He came back after three-quarters of an hour. The departure is again put off until morning. Fathers Frans Waldram and Willem Vissers will be accompanying them.

Wednesday, March 3

At quarter to three this afternoon: Two sisters, one brother, and two fathers have actually left for Bangassou. Everybody is happy, especially those who are leaving on furlough. For the first time in a long time, we were able to write a letter to our families.

Two trucks containing military police have left today for Dakwa and Ango. The population down there is revolting: at Dakwa, there is even a chief who is the head of it.

Thursday, March 4

Father Jan van Wagenberg had to interrupt his Mass: he is ill. His hand is swollen with a kind of worm infection. The sisters went to ask the colonel if he could be transported to Bangassou. The colonel is in immediate agreement but thinks it's too bad that a car had just left Bondo. It will be necessary to wait for the next opportunity.

Friday, March 5

An airplane flying very low and visibly in reconnaissance creates some panic.

Saturday, March 6

Father van Wagenberg will be able to depart as soon as the automobile that has left for Titule in order to get the sisters and Brother Jef has returned.[30] At least that is what has been promised us.

Sunday, March 7

In listening to the Masses that are broadcast on different stations of the radio, we are trying to learn some of the liturgical changes that have been put into effect.

Monday, March 8

The English miss from Banalia who had been taken back to her post a few days ago is again at the sisters'. Things are not going well down there. There are regular bombings, and there have been some quarrels among the Simba themselves.

At Nairobi, the two parties who are present find it difficult to understand each other.

Tuesday, March 9

Early in the morning: The soldiers bring seven black sisters to the convent. All this time they have been hiding in the woods, along the route that goes to Niangara. Their clothes are filthy and worn out, but they themselves look like they're doing well.

In the evening: The white sisters come over to give us a report on the seven black sisters. It seems like an adventurous novel from the Middle Ages.

At seven o'clock, we get a communication: we should stay

30 Ursuline Sisters Damiana Gielen, Lamberta Stelten, and Anna Gielen and Crosier Brother Jef Wouters had been taken by the rebels from Bili to Titule.

together, for the colonel is going to arrive with some big shot. We alert everybody right away, throw our habits on, and a little later, the colonel's black Mercedes arrives. We gather round because the big shot is going to speak. He presents himself as a commander who is conducting an inspection for General Olenga. He says he sees that we seem satisfied enough and under the good protection of the colonel. We give our approval to this. In finishing, he asks us for our papers. Then, they are going to discuss things with Bishop Mbali. In passing, the colonel says to Brother Leo (his personal friend, now that Brother Marcel is on furlough...): "All the Dutch are going to return to Bondo." We are accustomed to this sort of visit, and this doesn't disturb our peace. It seems that the colonel doesn't trouble himself any more about all that these big shots would like to see.

Thursday, March 11

Our papers, which had been taken, are now returned to us. This delegate of the general only speaks well of the fathers. The sisters please him less, because they have acted so freely as to even ask if they might all return to Europe.

For the swimmers, it's truly a glorious time. The water level has really gone up, and we have just been enjoying ourselves immensely. The fishers among us are also giving themselves up to what they love.

Saturday, March 13

For about two or three days now we have only been celebrating three personal Masses each day. The Mass wine has become rare. We are awaiting with impatience the return of Brother Jef, the sisters, and their two companions from Bangassou.

Yesterday, the Simba who came back from their expedition to Ango and Dakwa brought a tabernacle, a chalice, and some altar linen to the sisters' house. We think that the tabernacle comes from the sisters' chapel in Dakwa. All of this was found in the bushes alongside the road.

Monday, March 15

A reconnaissance plane creates, among us as well as among the Simba, the inevitable panic. When the plane made a second passage

Saint Augustine: 354–430

Spiritual Father of the Order of the Holy Cross
Feast Day, August 28

Saint Augustine, you grew up a child in Africa,
a down and out student and member of an off-beat religion,
often at odds with your mother, Saint Monica.
As a gifted but unhappy young adult, you were a "seeker" who studied and
taught philosophy. After your conversion to Christ,
you became a priest and bishop, a founder of a community
and writer of masterful theology to explain and defend Christianity.
You established a "rule" for religious community life.
For 800 years, the Crosiers have followed your way of life, placing
an emphasis on loving God and neighbor, on prayer,
and communal sharing. The crooked paths of your life encourage us,
Saint Augustine, to never doubt God's presence and love
in the ups and downs of our own lives.
Help us to believe that, despite our weaknesses, we are made
for greatness in this life and the life to come.
Through Christ our Lord.
Amen.

Author: Fr. Bob Rossi, osc

Crosier Martyrs de Bondo, 1964–1965

We praise you, Lord, for the courage of these Crosier "Martyrs of Charity." They faced death in 1964–65 rather than abandon the people of the Congo. May their blood be the seed of the Church in that still ravaged country.

Evangelizer of the poor **Fr. Joseph Beckers, osc, 49**
Formator of the native clergy **Fr. Robert Carremans, osc, 55**
Helpful man of action **Fr. Marion Godefrooy, osc, 52**
Teacher of professors and students **Fr. Victor Van Heeswijk, osc, 37**
Helper of the needy **Br. Leonard Ignoul, osc, 57**
Zealous baptizer of catechumens **Fr. Gerard Jensen, osc, 58**
Enthusiastic priest of ministry **Fr. Gerard Kester, osc, 47**
Benefactor of all **Fr. Godefried Raewinkels, osc, 43**
Selfless servant **Fr. Paul Kruitwagen, osc, 52**
Spiritual director of native religious and clergy **Fr. Alphonse Kuypers, osc, 40**
Prophet of Church renewal **Fr. Hubert Van Lieshout, osc, 31**
Kind friend of everyone **Fr. John Van Oort, osc, 38**
Exemplary religious and servant **Br. Lambert Schoenmakers, osc, 47**
Animator of youth **Fr. Henry Snijkers, osc, 37**
Enthusiastic witness of joy **Fr. Albert Timmers, osc, 35**
Confrere radiating joy **Fr. Henry Verberk, osc, 47**
Apostle of youth **Fr. John Verhoeven, osc, 31**
Zealous wise man for all **Br. Peter Verkuylen, osc, 66**
Counselor with good sense **Fr. Arnold Vervoort, osc, 40**
Saint committed to everything **Fr. William Vissers, osc, 55**
Revealer of God's love **Fr. Philip Waldram, osc, 54**
Shy man of courage **Fr. William Van Wetten, osc, 45**
Builder of churches and friendship **Br. Joseph Wouters, osc, 59**

1210 2010
Starting Afresh
From A *Place of Light*

over Buta, a few hundred Simba emptied their rifles. The D.C.A, of which we are always afraid, intervenes too late. Immediately after the plane vanishes, the Simba rush down to the airport runway, where they find another four victims of their madness: four cows were grazing there. It's too bad that they wounded the bull. He too is finished off.

Tuesday, March 16

We are awaiting, day by day with more impatience, the return of those who went to Titule and to Bangassou. Our meals are getting more and more spare.

In the evening: We learn by way of Radio Brussels that Brother Marcel and the two sisters have arrived at Zaventem in Europe where they are welcomed by Bishop Creemers and the provincial of the Crosiers, Dr. A. Ramaekers.

Wednesday, March 17

After coffee break: Great news—Brother Jef and the sisters from Bili have arrived. Brother Jef came hurriedly to our house and is welcomed with open arms. He passed through some difficult moments and even narrowly escaped being killed on January 18. It was the anniversary of the death of Lumumba, and this coincided with the announcement of the fall of Bondo. The sisters had been warned and fled into the woods. The Simba, drunk and making merry, had imprisoned all the soldiers favorable to the mission and would have killed everybody if a commander had not arrived on the spot just in time to restore order.

For the moment, says Brother Jef, panic reigns among the populations of Dakwa and Ango. The military organize raids where everybody is killed right on the spot. The villages have been abandoned, and everybody is hiding in the woods.

Thursday, March 18

Three sisters from Bili come to see us before noon. They are skinny and still nervous. This is their tragic-comic story: during the night, a drunk Simba dressed in a chasuble arrives at the sisters' house. He has a radio under his arm. He comes, he says, as a priest so that they can make their confessions to him. He will read a Mass the next day. The sisters, full of fear, kept him there for a full hour until he gave a thousand francs to each one of them, and then he went away...

Tony, the Swiss man who is supposed to set up the trip to Bondo, comes after dinner. None of the fathers who are at Bangassou has yet to arrive. We don't understand any of it. They have a pass for a furlough of two weeks, and they should be showing up. This could cause us some difficulties.

In the evening: There is a communiqué from Radio Hilversum: The Crosiers of Buta occupy a special position, if one compares them with the other groups of fathers living in the Territory held by the rebels.

Friday, March 19

The sisters have received a letter from the whites in Bondo: Fathers Willem Vissers and Frans Waldram had been on the road until they came to Bangui, and they will come back with provisions for the white population of Bondo. We await their return this week.

Saturday, March 20

The sisters tell us that there is a good chance that Sister Narcissa and Father van Wagenberg might obtain today their permit of passage. Brother Willem Tieken would like to accompany them, for he seems to suffer from a cancer of the skin.

They go to the colonel's house before noon, but they wait in vain for forty-five minutes. The colonel is nowhere to be found.

Sunday, March 21

There are few people at Mass this morning. Rumors are circulating among the population that the National Congolese Army might be approaching. People were already taking flight, but the Simba stopped them.

In the evening: We are dismayed by a sorrowful screaming at the sisters' house. A little later, we learn the reason: the colonel came and forced a black sister, Sister Josepha, to go with him. Did she let herself be taken? We don't have the final word on it, but in any case it is a difficult blow for the sisters. There exists a danger now: might the other officers do the same? We are all a little somber this evening.

Tuesday, March 23

The diocesan priest Father Joseph of Balele has arrived here. There also, the house and the church were pillaged while he watched. He had been staying there all this time. Bishop Jacques of Buta now has a good portion of his priests here.

Wednesday, March 24

They say that Sister Narcissa can leave, but not the fathers, because the two other fathers have not come back yet from Bangassou.

The colonel showed up at the sisters' again last night, and they read him the riot act because of his behavior with Sister Josepha. He was not very pleased.

Thursday, March 25

According to the diocesan priest Father Marcel, three hundred men from here who should have been sent to Aba for training ended up being imprisoned there by General Olenga. Their officers were likewise imprisoned. Brother Venance saw this morning the bodies of the Simba who were executed; they were slain because they had given some powder to their parents for hunting.

Saturday, March 27

In the evening the colonel comes to relax in a little motor boat on the Rubi. He has his worries, he says. And it's true. From the strategic point of view, his position is ridiculous. He would like to go to Aba, but his officers advise him against it, for the general does not seem too fond of the Simba from Buta. He cannot attack Stanleyville, because he would encounter the Simba of Banalia, with whom he has already had enough trouble. And Zobia is occupied by the "enemy" Simba. To depart for Paulis doesn't make sense either, because another "boss" is there as well. It follows that he has to stay here. There is nothing going on.

In the evening: We learn that, according to the officers, it is

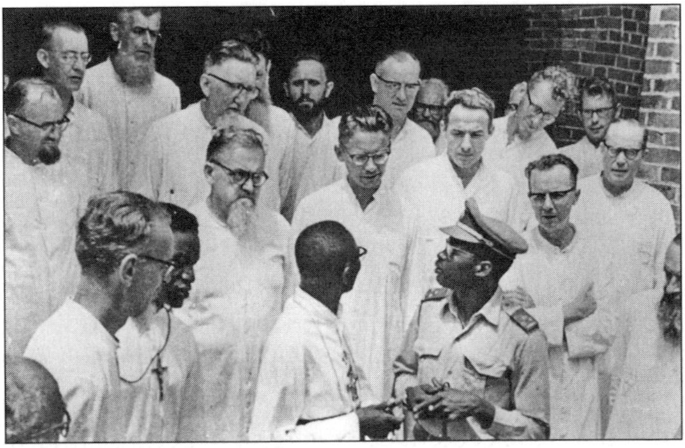

The hostages in Buta with Colonel Augustine Makondo.
(Photo courtesy of the Crosier Province of Blessed Theodore de Celles, Europe.)

possible for two fathers to depart but only one sister. The other sisters have to come back from their furlough first. We don't understand any of it.

SUNDAY, MARCH 28

After the High Mass, the colonel tells Brother Leo that he has received a promotion. They are saying that Gbenye would personally name him lieutenant-general. Brother Leo will also be able to depart on furlough, the colonel says.

We learn from the sisters that the car that should transport the sick to Bangassou has already departed. The black sisters think that the head of the expedition, a Sudanese who is against whites, has forgotten them on purpose.

After dinner: A Simba comes to tell us that the two fathers from Bangassou are in Bondo and will arrive here very shortly.

TUESDAY, MARCH 30

During these last days, the National Congolese Army has really made progress: Aru, Aba, Faradje, and Watsa have fallen. The radio also communicated that three whites have been liberated at Watsa. This is a favorable communication for us and our future. We really feel, though, that the moment of our liberation will be very dangerous.

The colonel comes to us very late in the afternoon (he is in a very discouraged mood). He asks if we can lodge here a Portuguese man along with his wife and children. The colonel really is in a very somber mood, for a communiqué has announced that Aketi and Ndulia have been bombed.

At six thirty, a big truck arrives with the fathers from Bangassou and a fabulous cargo of provisions. We are happy to the point of being silly.

It seems that the Marists of Buta, who are now still at Bangui, are our benefactors. Moreover, each one had put something of his own inside to help us. One would believe that the whole world lives with us and that efforts are being made everywhere to liberate us. The Capuchin fathers who have come back from furlough spontaneously gave over their provisions of cigarettes, tobacco, and other delicacies.

The colonel arrives soon with the Portuguese family. We offer him a bottle of whiskey. What a lively spirit in the mission, and everybody has some news to report.

Wednesday, March 31

In the afternoon, we hear that, when the little bridge is restored between Buta and Bondo, a convoy of whites will depart for Bangassou; among them will be the Portuguese family, Father van Wagenberg and Brother Willem, the Garcia family of Bondo, and one sister.

Thursday, April 1

Late in the afternoon: The convoy of whites, of which I spoke yesterday, did indeed depart. Wonderful! It's said that Brother Leo will be able to leave on furlough tomorrow. One speaks at the same time of a plan according to which a new group would be sent to Bangassou to seek a new shipment of medicines, while some of the fathers would go to exercise an apostolate during Easter time at Monga.

Sunday, April 4

One of the junior Marist brothers comes to report a story that is circulating among the Simba about the attack on Stanleyville that is always being postponed. About fifteen days ago, a strong group of about thirty rebels was en route for Stanleyville to scout around the area. While on the road, they saw five Jews, big and black, right on the road ahead of them (the commandos who took Watsa, Faradja, and Aba had received training in Israel). The Simba started firing on the five of them, but they didn't move in the slightest. The rebels began approaching them, all the time firing on them. The Jews were paying no attention and just looked in the direction of the firing. Nothing but that! When the rebels drew closer to the Jews, the fattest Jew among them came up and took one of the Simba by his leg and "ripped it off" from top to bottom (this is the truth according to the narrators…). He threw the two halves of the unfortunate one—one to the right and one to the left—in the bushes. Panicked, the twenty-nine others fled into the forest, and now there is no one who wants to march on Stanleyville.

Monday, April 5

Brother Leo went to the office to get his permission to leave. The secretary said that Brother Leo would indeed be able to depart but not the others.

In the evening, Bishop Jacques gives us a "speech" in the dining room. We should be more prudent in our actions here at the mission. We are not yet entirely "out of danger," and we should avoid anything that would send the Simba's blood pressure up. We shouldn't forget that many hate us, that many have learned to hate us. There are many little selfish things that make them angry at us. Now that there are hardly any cigarettes left in Buta, we shouldn't walk around all the time with something between our lips and act as if all the world belonged to us. When the sisters are here, we cannot laugh at our ease. That irritates them and makes them think of the colonial days, during which the whites considered the Congo their own country. We should not put on an air of well-being among the Simba who are worked up and who are acquainted with a lot of misery and suffering. We should take account of the fact that, for the moment, they are putting up with us and nothing more...Brother Leo has not yet departed.

After dinner, a plane passes over close enough to shave the turf at the mission, and that creates an infernal noise. A little after, the Simba start singing everywhere. We notice a little later that there are some notices scattered in the sisters' garden. The Simba gather them up and read the name of General Olenga, and they think that the general himself was in the plane. In fact, it's a question of a propaganda trick. Later, we are able to read one of the papers. On the left upper corner, there was a portrait of Mama Ohema, the personal witch doctor of General Olenga. She declares in this text that she puts all her force and all her power at the service of the central government and asks the Simba to surrender.

In the evening, we learn that Father van Wagenberg and Brother Willem Tieken arrived last Monday in Bangassou.

Thursday, April 8

Around ten o'clock: The colonel personally brings over the permit for Brother Leo to depart. Now he has to wait for a car that will be departing in the direction of Bondo.

In the evening: We nervously follow the military communiqués: Ndungu and Niangara have fallen.

Friday, April 9

Fifteen people were again executed yesterday evening. There had been twenty-one accused, and six were acquitted. One of the fifteen came up, still alive, out of the water and was then cared for at the hospital.

During dinner: The Simba bring over a Cypriot, who owns a plantation in Kulu, between Likati and Bondo. A plane had surveyed his house, and the Simba suspected that he had a ham radio. They found a photo developer at the house and led him to the colonel at Buta. Fortunately, the colonel knew what it was, and the man was set free.

Around five o'clock: He returns home after Brother Lambert gave him some provisions. It must be very difficult for those who live alone like that.

Saturday, April 10

Yesterday evening: An assembly was suddenly sounded. According to the sisters, this is what was discussed: Gbenye and the general would be in the forest around Ndungu. The Simba of Buta are going to free them. Nevertheless, the colonel is staying here. Fortunately for us.

In mid-morning: The Simba come to get seven cows. The reason: the general will be here a few days and there will be a big feast.

Sunday, April 11

Today, some posters were put up inviting the fathers to assist at a football match.

Almost everybody set out for the football field around four o'clock. One would've wished to avoid that. Everywhere on the road we met friendly faces, and we had to jump to the side to avoid the cars of the officers flying through like missiles. Having arrived there (the sisters had been brought in a car), we were led to the reviewing stand to take the places of honor. Augustine was there also, with Patricia (Sister Josepha). The show started with a demonstration of Judo by the commandos, which was more comical than impressive, but even so received some spontaneous applause. Then the football game began. A wretched game. In the meantime we were treated to the cacophony of a band that was "playing" in a corner of the review stand. They weren't bad; it even sounded good, if you took into account the fact that they had never been taught. The director was a master showman, and when he saw that we were enjoying it, he "went to town" to amuse us. In the end, we were watching the band perform more than the players on the field who were playing terribly. Altogether it was amusing, and it was a pleasant atmosphere.

At the end of the game, "Gus," the colonel, became excited (he appeared to be nervous) and began to distribute instructions to some officers who were armed to the teeth. What was going to happen yet? Then began an exercise that was worthwhile. Everybody had to leave the edges of the field. About twenty Simba began to march around the field, and an imaginary combat with bullets followed. It was very exciting. In the end, they threw themselves into hand-to-hand combat in which Augustine, to be sure, played the role of the hero... At a certain moment, Augustine seemed to be hurt in the head. And the exercise ended.

After staying seated for a moment in the grass with his head in his hands, Augustine, getting up and with sweat pouring out all over, came over to us to shake our hands. We got back home, just as satisfied as kids who had come home after a long trip. On the road coming back, everybody again showed themselves to be very friendly, which made us feel very good.

Five truckloads of soldiers left again, yesterday and today, in the direction of Niangara.

Monday, April 12

Patricia seems to be a good influence on the colonel. It seems that he is very dangerous when he is in a very bad mood. Then, he has to have some victims, and since there are always some members of RADECO in prison, the victims are quickly found.

That happened again one or two days ago. He had five come out of the prison. When he wished to slay them, Patricia began to weep and to cry out, so much so that the colonel found his better feelings and counseled them to flee into the forest and to never appear again!

Tuesday, April 13

The sisters inform us of the arrival in Buta, one or two days ago, of the Simba who had killed the fathers at Dakwa. The colonel wanted to slay him immediately, but the officers protested. So, he sent him to the front in the direction of Doruma.

When it is already late in the evening, there are the sounds of a celebration: the mother of the colonel has arrived.

Wednesday, April 14

Preparations for Holy Week are beginning at church: confessions and practices for the ceremonies.

The radio announces that the "Jews" have arrived at just the right moment: they were able to take off with two hundred thousand liters of gas, twenty new trucks, and more than a thousand prisoners.

In the evening: The colonel comes to introduce us to his mother. A beautiful person. When she goes to see the bishop, the colonel stays with us and talks a bit. He complains of the Europeans who leave on furlough and who don't come back. He cites the Reverend Paul who is already in Norway with his whole family. He thinks that's a mistake. He would not touch the whites. He has always protected them. He will continue to do so. We shouldn't believe that he would slay us at the last moment, when the Americans will arrive here. He would let them come and would say to them: "The fathers are there, safe and sound. I preserved them very well."

Holy Thursday

After dinner: Some of the diocesan priests leave with the holy oils for Likati and Bondo. The bishop had blessed the oils early in the morning.

The ceremonies begin at four thirty in the afternoon. There are a lot of people, and everything goes very well.

Good Friday

Again, lots of people at the service, which is very simple.

Holy Saturday

A group of Simba clean up in front of the church. Ceremonies are in the evening.

Easter

Brother Leo should have left yesterday, but nothing happened. We reflect today, with a certain lump in our throats, on all the missionary posts where the people are not able to celebrate their Easter. In all this huge territory, it is only Bondo and Buta that celebrate today.

We estimate that there were about three thousand people at church for the Masses.

From the people, we learn that Gbenye and the general would already be at Buta but wanted to stay a few days out of reach. Is there something true in this news?

One says also that the "wet" Simba (former soldiers of the National Congolese Army who are ready to pass to the other side) have sent a message to the others, asking them to take off.

Easter Monday

Early in the morning, the rebels come here with thirteen cows. Three of them are for us. They come from Poko and look to be in terrible shape.

Commander Gustave comes and asks us to save his money for him. After having consulted the diocesan priests, we don't dare accept it.

Tony tells us that the tension is mounting among the Simba. Some of the leaders of Stanleyville have taken refuge here, and this is creating some quarrels. Yesterday, they had to "empty out" the bar because of fights.

Tuesday, April 20

For a day or two now, we have no light. The man who was in charge went to see the bishop. He wanted to flee for his life since there are difficulties now at the electrical plant. The bishop asked him to stay on.

The radio announces that Basoko, the hometown of Augustine, has been taken.

In the evening: The diocesan priests come back from Likati. There and at Bondo, everything is peaceful. The sisters come again with some news. The soldiers who had departed for Niangara have suddenly come back. The population there is against them and had alerted the National Congolese Army. This did not make the colonel very happy. The officers of this group came back last night after having waited for several days. This morning, having called them, the colonel expressed his anger at them. He wanted to slay them all on the spot, but a major had been able to take hold of his hands, and he let his rifle fall. Then Augustine broke down in sobs. From the diocesan priests, we learn how the terror is mounting in Buta. Some people have begun again to denounce people of whom they are afraid, in case of the arrival of the National Congolese Army.

Wednesday, April 21

Brother Venance reports that, again yesterday, the colonel forbade the soldiers to come and to "hang out" with no purpose here at the mission or in the vicinity. If somebody does it anyway, he will kill him on the spot.

The colonel was again in an excellent mood yesterday evening. He met a woman someplace on the road who was about to give birth. He entered immediately into action, offered his car to transport her to the hospital, and went to alert the sisters. He came himself to wait then at the door. A little later, when everything had transpired very well, the sisters named the kid "Augustine," and the colonel was in seventh heaven.

Thursday, April 22

These last days, several truckloads of Simba have departed in the direction of Paulis. This group will certainly not dare risk to suddenly return! The sisters have told us that the number of victims of the People's Court keeps growing. It could count several hundred.

Radio Hilversum was announcing yesterday evening that Father

Jan Smit, osc, who might have been killed in New Guinea during a rebellion against the Indochinese government, had in fact been killed for reasons of personal animosity.

This evening: We learn by radio that Father Jan van Wagenberg and "Father" Willem Tieken, who had their apostolate in the province of Buta, have arrived in Europe and can take a furlough of undetermined length. The communication is spreading everywhere.

Saturday, April 24

Brother Leo and Tony are occupied with repairing the central electric plant. There they learn from the colonel that they must absolutely continue their work, for President Gbenye will arrive this evening yet.

Later in the afternoon: We notice a few things which say, in effect, that something is going to happen. Again, trucks are going around, and the Simba are repairing the roads; two hundred twenty ferry-boatloads of beer have arrived.

Sunday, April 25

We are awakened at four o'clock in the morning by the shooting of mortars. At first, we thought that Gbenye had arrived.

It seems that that's what it was alright. In mid-morning there is a big parade. Some of the diocesan priests go to watch. Gbenye doesn't give a speech to the soldiers. Anyway, what could he say?

In the afternoon: We learn already some "opinions" of the great master. He is very content with the colonel because he has so well-protected the fathers and the sisters. They would like to see the schools open. If there is not enough space, we could use the method of teaching boys and girls together.

A Te Deum is scheduled for tomorrow morning. We will see.

Monday, April 26

Very early already, the sisters come to warn us that the Te Deum will take place at eight o'clock precisely. The church is decorated, some additional chairs with some cushions have been brought over, and we practice the Te Deum one time.

About eight o'clock, a group of about forty soldiers takes position in the main aisle of the church. Everybody is ready. We, the fathers, are in the choir. The sisters are further back in the church. There is no one else in the rest of the church.

A little later, the fanfare begins. We wait until five minutes to nine. Then, some cars arrive; the bell sounds; the soldiers present their arms; and we, leaning on the railing, look at the procession entering the church. Christophe Gbenye, president of the new revolutionary government, seems to look a little like Fidel Castro: dressed in khaki with gym shoes into which he has tucked the cuffs of his pants. A serious face outlined by a thick black beard. Augustine is wearing a long Arab costume. The other majors and officers are all dressed in differing ways. The carnival-type procession proceeds thus toward the altar. The flourish of trumpets begins a popular hymn used throughout the church. Bishop Jacques, assisted by two black priests, intones the Te Deum. Gbenye begins to pray his rosary. After the ceremony, a noisy exit of "the gladiators" from the church. Outside, Gbenye shakes hands with the bishop and promises to pass by the mission after his lunch.

We wait until noon, eating a half-hour earlier, and his lordship comes royally at three o'clock. Several officers and "favored ones" accompany him. His guard arrives a little later. Augustine is not there. It seems that he's ill. We all go down and shake hands with the president and stand around the front door. No one knows what to say...Gbenye speaks a little with the bishop and the diocesan priests. The bishop asks him if he will speak a little with the fathers. He comes closer to us and begins to talk softly, fast, and in a perfect French; seen close up, he gives a fairly friendly impression, especially because of his expressive eyes.

Here is a little of the content of his "speech." He had been in Belgium, and there he noticed that there is a lot of negative reporting of his movement. The newspapers treat both himself and his men as communists and murderers. There is no truth in it. And more, they are not against religion nor are they against the missionaries. He knows that there have been some victims, but we should consider those as "special cases," something that happens everywhere during troubled times. He has never wanted that. And then: we missionaries are there for idealism. We want to make sacrifices and they should be made; at times, even the sacrifice of martyrdom, thanks to which we will fly to heaven like arrows. That is what, after all, we teach the people. He is not against us but against Belgium. Spaak is not a nice man; he plays a double game, that which is proven by the large amount of paratroopers in Stanleyville. Spaak is a Freemason. Gbenye has not been against us; he has arrived now to ask for our prayers. Certainly, we should pray for him. "You should pray much for us. If we are on the wrong road, your prayers will convert us; if we are on the right road, your prayers will give us victory." When the allocution was finished, we applauded without holding back…

We all came forward, for they were going to take a picture of the group: Gbenye and the bishop in the middle of a group of fathers. Then the president accompanied the bishop to his room, and we retired. A little later, the bishop quickly came to us to inform us of their discussion. The bishop was fairly direct in what he said, and the president had to swallow it! The bishop told him: "I am not against your politics, nor against your party, but I must protest the fashion in which you are proceeding. To kill your political enemies is not good politics. To destroy everything everywhere, that is not the liberation of the people. And again, here in Buta where there are so many people murdered yet! Because of the People's Court, there reigns a terrible fear that is degenerating into hate! And the fathers who are at the mission! They are doing nothing here. Many of them are young, they want to work, and they can't do anything. They just vegetate here, and even that isn't going so well, for we find it difficult to find food. They are here like hostages." Gbenye denied that. We were absolutely free. For the rest, Gbenye had nothing to say except to nod his head affirmatively! He would think about all that and come back another time.

And then, the whole group withdrew.

In the evening: We learn that the colonel is not at all ill. He was at the sisters', and he was livelier than ever. He was feeling particularly "high," and as usual, when there are other officers present, he acts as if that isn't to be noticed.

At the black sisters', Gbenye insisted that the black sisters who are hiding in the forest should be sought out. His niece is one of them. No one dared to inform him that those sisters are already in

Leopoldville.

The white sisters have learned from a Simba how the soldiers celebrated Easter at Baye. They had placed a statue of the Virgin in the middle of the sisters' chapel and surrounded it with candles. They then prayed and sang. A few had put on some priestly vestments and were lording it over the others…At the end, they put some beds around the statue, to have a guard for the night. Suddenly, at midnight, the pews began to dance, and they all fled.

Tuesday, April 27

All kinds of news has come to us especially by means of the black sisters. Augustine was particularly high yesterday. One hears (Patricia knows it all) that it's rumored among the Simba that Gbenye is not absolutely in agreement with the protection that has been given to us by Augustine. Gbenye would have slain all the sisters and all the fathers immediately after his arrival here. But now, he can brag that he spared us. Augustine has not only been in a good mood, he has also been in a religious mood. Yesterday evening, he went to chapel with all the sisters. He got down on the prie-dieu of the bishop and stayed there so long that finally the sister superior had to go over to him and tell him that that was enough. Gbenye had also come to the sisters' chapel and had asked for one of the relics that were to be found in the altar stone. The sisters told him that they could not give it to him. One of the white sisters then remarked that he would do better to go to Banalia where there were so many missionaries that were killed. In the meantime, it seems that the wife of Gbenye has taken off. She's had enough of being afraid and of hiding in the forest, and she's now left. Is it for that reason that Augustine did not introduce "his Patricia" to the president?

Patricia told the sisters that she had asked Augustine to pray before and after they eat a meal together. He does it now. So, she seems to have some influence on him. It is fortunate, both for the sisters and for us, that "that has stopped" with Patricia. There are no other sisters who are harassed, and it's much calmer at the sisters' mission since Augustine doesn't have to come and court Sister Josepha.

And so continues this Middle Ages-like novel that is unfolding for the moment here at Buta.

Thursday, April 29

Yesterday and today, the city has been very agitated. All day long, they've been practicing with machine guns. Some say that an attack against Stanleyville is in the works. It seems that the colonel, in the midst of a meeting, had addressed himself to the president, in a fairly blunt manner, on the subject of promised reinforcements that come too late. People are saying that Ngai and Muma have fallen. In the meantime, a horse has arrived here, the one belonging to Nunes, a Portuguese man who was assassinated at Dakwa. He was brought here tied up in a truck and is really a pity to see.

After dinner: We are awaiting the visit of Gbenye about five o'clock. Even though he had promised, he doesn't show up. In the evening, the generator for electricity is again not functioning.

Friday, April 30

Jean de Strooper, who has come back from an expedition to inspect the bridges (and to accumulate a stock of coffee), has brought us a chalice from our mission post at Api. It was in the possession of the president of the party in a village and was offered to him.

Saturday, May 1

The pope writes an encyclical on the subject of world peace that is so threatened.

At noon: We have, for the first time this week, meat again for dinner. There's so little, there will be no more question of it, for they have used up the last cows for the event of the arrival of Gbenye.

Despite the presence of the president, there is little news, little hope of a quick liberation (moreover, it doesn't matter who one might be), little hope of a future, and no...light.

One of the generators jumped out of place. The principal mechanic is in the hospital with wounds on his head.

The diocesan priests tell us that Gbenye has spoken to the Simba about being more moderate in their treatment of the civilians. There will be no more assassinations of civilians. The possessions of the members of RADECO who were killed should be returned to their

A group of Crosiers, together with a few Brothers of Saint Gabriel and Capuchins standing in back of the bishop's house at Buta where they were killed on May 30, 1965, by the rebels.

(Photo courtesy of the Crosier Province of Blessed Theodore de Celles, Europe.)

families and not kept by the Simba themselves.

Sunday, May 2

A very agitated Sunday morning. At quarter to seven already, the colonel (still in his pajamas so to speak) brings over a package coming from Bondo, and he says to Brother Leo that he should be ready to depart immediately for Bangassou. Father Godefrooy and Brother Lambert should accompany him in order to go to Baye to print some papers for the Simba.

So, all morning we are awaiting this immediate departure. In the meantime, we learn that Bondo is in the hands of the Congolese National Army. It's probably not true, but even so that elevates the "temperature" of the region. So it is no longer interesting to go to Baye.

In the afternoon: The travelers are still waiting. We learn in the meantime that the "doughnut"[31] has left during the night. There are also some wounded who have arrived from Aketi. In the same way, some starving people arrive from the region of Stanleyville. Misery must reign down there. Gbenye asked the colonel to transport these miserable people here, but the colonel doesn't see any possibility of caring for them on a grand scale.

At ten minutes before six: A well-loaded truck finally arrives here at the mission to take along the travelers. The diocesan priest Father Marcel is also on this trip. It seems that he must leave to have an operation. Such a departure, of one of us who can return to his own place, brings with it each time a strange kind of emotion. The driver says that the colonel is also making the trip but in a luxury car.

Monday, May 3

In the afternoon: The sisters tell us that the colonel has made known to Patricia (by telephone) that they have arrived in Bondo and that everything is "fine." We learn also that a whole series of vehicles has departed. They are even speaking of five trucks of armed Simba. That should signify that there really is something going on down there. The bishop says that he is sure that the National Congolese Army is on the Bili at Monga.

---

31 The French word for doughnut is *beignet* and rhymes with Gbenye.

Patricia brings us a letter with one thousand francs. This is for Masses for the colonel, for he will be in danger.

In the evening, again the electricity is out, but then the motor was up and running again.

Wednesday, May 5

The colonel's mother came over to the sisters' yesterday evening to say that her son sent a telegram to announce that the "operation" had fully succeeded: they drove back the "wet ones" all the way to Yakoma. At Monga, they were able to seize three trucks and two jeeps, booty that they will soon show off in Buta. What should we believe?

At this moment, the most fantastic stories are circulating on the subject of what happened down there. Thirty-six trucks had left Buta for this attack along with three pieces of artillery and an incalculable number of Simba.

As for us, we are thinking of another possibility: it could be a question of a camouflage of a transport of coffee and ivory for Bangassou.

A general consideration: when Aba, Watsa, and Faradje were taken, one after the other and at an accelerated cadence, we had thought here at Buta that it was only a question of a few weeks. Now, we have again lost that hope. We have more and more the impression that they will not attack Buta (and will not effectuate a bombing from the air) because they are afraid for our lives.

The mood that reigns right now among us is difficult to describe: is it indifference or simply a sort of depression?

It appears, in the meantime, that the visit of Gbenye was not harmful to us. They are no longer destroying the desks in the schools, and the Simba seem friendlier than ever. We are beginning to take walks along the tranquil paths surrounding the mission. The bishop went for a walk yesterday for the first time on the highway. It's the first time that he has dared something of that sort among the population.

In the afternoon: A young man informs us that the famous battle did not take place in the vicinity of Monga but rather around Faka (near Lobi). That would signify that Monga is in the hands of the

National Congolese Army. We know in fact only very little on the subject of the exact circumstances and have to await the return of the colonel. Twelve very badly wounded have already arrived here, which indicates that it was really a savage fight, wherever it was. As usual, there were no higher officers among the wounded...The sisters have the impression that the Simba who were at the hospital are very demoralized.

Thursday, May 6

In the evening: The sisters inform us that the general from Banalia who was demoted here and has been in prison has escaped. As "compensation," some of the jailors have already been slain. We are fearful that the colonel, who is due to arrive tonight around nine o'clock, might make some more victims.

Some of the fathers were going to go for a walk today after coffee. They were in civilian clothing and were walking along the wooded paths around the mission farm. Just as they arrived at the highway, a car came flying at high speed toward them. A captain got out, smiled, and then said: "You are certainly some of the fathers?" We could not but say that he was right. He had been warned, among other things, that a group of mercenaries was walking through the woods.

Friday, May 7

According to the news, the colonel did come back last night. According to one of the Simba, the "wet ones" had undergone some heavy losses "in the bath." Some whites were also killed. The colonel declared this morning at assembly that he had pushed back the National Congolese Army about 125 miles.

In the evening: Radio Leopoldville announces that Monga is in the hands of government soldiers.

During the evening broadcasts, Radio Leopoldville repeated the communiqué of yesterday: that the National Congolese Army had liberated Monga and was operating now in that region.

One of the black sisters spoke yesterday with the colonel, who stated that the fathers and brothers who had left here were still in Bondo.

Early in the morning, a mother accompanied by her seven children came to pay a visit to the bishop. A beautiful family to behold. The man who accompanied them was not the father but an uncle. The father had been slain at Buta. The bishop and the diocesan priests were very moved as they welcomed the family. For them, more than for us, this is a terrible time. They know all the people. Often, the victims are among the better parishioners and those who do good.

After dinner: We learn that the car in which Gbenye had departed is again in Buta. It seems that they had run into some difficulties on the way, and the driver has come back and has given his report. They were part of a column of two trucks and the colonel's Mercedes, en route for Doruma. At a certain place, they were surprised by a patrol of the National Congolese Army. Gbenye was able to flee.

In the evening: Radio Leopoldville confirms that Monga is in the hands of government troops while the people have received provisions of food and medicine.

Sunday, May 9

There's more and more news making the rounds. The worst is that Mr. Garcia has been killed at Bondo. The story is very complicated. The colonel went to Ndu; he wanted to pass over the river, and on the other side a crowd began to gather. He could not get over, he got angry, but he was finally able to contact a relative of Garcia. This man proposed the passage of his family as a condition of a certain transaction. This excited the colonel against him. At Bondo, he took out his anger against the family of Garcia. He badly treated Garcia. Then, it seems that a little afterward, some officers killed him. This news has again demoralized us.

About eleven o'clock: The Simba came and put up a poster inviting all of us to a football game to be played in honor of Colonel Augustine, who brought off at Monga a stunning victory over the forces of the National Congolese Army.

At four o'clock: We go down to the football field. First, there is a game between two teams of little girls, after which a girl rendered homage to the colonel for his courage and wished him the strength and power of God for the future—especially for the attack against Stanleyville, which ought to take place soon. Then the real game began. Again there was a flourish of trumpets, but this time one was not able to establish the same mood as the other day. We have the strong impression that the "lions" are depressed. Nothing could be seen that indicated that they would be celebrating a victory. Nevertheless, everyone was very friendly toward us. On the way back, it started to rain, and a car took us quickly back to the mission.

In the evening: Radio Leopoldville announces that Monga had fallen two days ago. This practically gives us the moral certitude that Monga, even if it was partially occupied by the Simba, is now certainly in the hands of the National Congolese Army.

Tuesday, May 11

After dinner, Jean de Strooper comes to say good-bye. He is departing immediately for Bangassou for a furlough of two months. This news plunges us into incertitude. Normally, we would have to conclude that Monga is even so still in the hands of the Simba. It's enough to make one sick. This is already the third time that we have been fooled by news from Radio Leopoldville.

We wonder also how and when Brother Marcel and Sister Paula will come back. What do they know about Monga? In any case, their permission to be on vacation has expired.

Thursday, May 13

Before noon: Marcel, a "lion" and relative of one of the black sisters who often comes to visit us, brings us a calendar for 1965. It was printed at Baye. On the bottom, one finds printed: *Makondo Augustine, the one and only.* We had already learned that Father Godefrooy was not able to do anything at Baye because everything had been destroyed. So this information then would be false.

At the end of the afternoon: Two fifteen-ton trucks arrive here loaded with thirteen cows. The animals are very skinny, and they have been on the trucks for one week, so say the "lions." They will remain there all night, and this evening, six guards arrive who will be on patrol near the trucks all night long.

Tony, the Swiss, comes again to visit us. He is in a somber mood because of the murder of Garcia. He also recounts that the Simba have brought back a prisoner, who was talking in the bar and saying that one hundred sixty men had left from Yakoma. They should continue in the direction of Bondo and leave a force of sixty men there and attack Buta with the rest. If any of this is true, that means the hierarchy of the National Congolese Army is not at all aware of the situation here.

Friday, May 14

All day long, there was a lot of going and coming here, all occasioned by the transport of the cows that were finally placed on the farm and will soon be slaughtered.

Saturday, May 15

In the evening: The Simba bring us some boxes of powdered milk that were given to them by Brother Lambert. On the other hand, they have no news. It will be necessary that we return soon to Bangassou, for our reserve in necessary provisions is rapidly diminishing.

In the evening: Radio Leopoldville announces that Mobutu has arrived at Bumba and they are preparing to make the connection with Stanleyville by way of Aketi and Buta. It's already a few months since they have spoken about this…

Here at Buta, they say that there is fighting at Poko and that the National Congolese Army has taken Bandoki. The mood among us, which has been really low these last days, is perking up a bit.

Sunday, May 16

This whole day there was going to be a lot of movement. At nine o'clock, there was going to be celebrated a solemn office for all the dead. It didn't come off, because it's Sunday. On the program, there was also the changing of the names of all the streets. All the names that call to mind the colonial period have to be changed. And so the name of Monsignor Dirks will disappear to give place to Monsignor Jacques. But this point on the program also had to be abandoned, or at least postponed to tomorrow. They are playing football again today, and we are again invited.

Then, after dinner, when we wanted to go down for the match, there was again a fair amount of confusion because of a burial that was being held with the beating of drums. We were not able to find one of the diocesan priests, and that made the Simba angry. One of us went to the church, and calm reigns again. A little afterward, we learned who was being buried. It was an officer who was admitted to the hospital thanks to a nurse who was on their side. He died a little later. The reason for the fight: a young woman.

At eleven o'clock, the call comes. The assassin was slain.

At three o'clock, we go to the match. Having arrived, we are immediately invited to the stands. The mood among the "lions" is excellent. They've been drinking a lot. The flourish of trumpets is grand also, and there's even a typed program of events that is handed to us. The colonel arrives a little late with his "harem," Patricia among them...They receive places of honor. Patricia is dressed like a flirt. The other "courtesans" don't really look respectable, and they certainly have nothing in common with the members of the Congregation of Mary...

The colonel is also in particularly good humor. All of the players on the field are more or less good players. Among them are some majors, a lot of officers, and some commanders. They don't play badly, but at times they commit such errors that make all of us in the stands laugh. The match is commented on by microphone, and then a little later, the colonel announces that there will be a Requiem Mass tomorrow for all those who have been killed. Everyone is invited. Dusk is upon us when we hit the road to go home. We hadn't gotten very far when a luxurious car stops alongside us and we are invited to get in. A second group of fathers is also taken in another car, so that ten of us are now flying back to the mission with some Simba situated on top of the cars. It wasn't yet totally dark, so we were able to dive into the river to take off some of the dust of the road and especially the fatigue of the long day.

Monday, May 17

The Solemn Requiem Mass started a half-hour late. A hundred or so soldiers were already both within and without the church about forty-five minutes before and presented their arms at the arrival of the military staff. The colonel was again well "decorated." The brass combo, which was with us in the nave of the church, reserved for him a welcome of "honor." The service began. During the consecration, the brass combo played the national anthem. Everything passed in good order, and the mood was good. After the Mass: the same ceremonial with the trumpets and the guard. A very audible order was given at the end that sounded a "comic note": "Geef acht!"[32] "Now take care of yourselves!" So, there are also some jokers among the "lions!"

32 In Flemish in the original text.

PART THREE

By Brother Lambert Schoenmakers, osc

After the taking of Buta on June 1, 1965, there were very few things found that belonged to the victims of May 30. Before fleeing, the Simba had emptied the buildings of the mission.

But on June 13, the chaplain, Belinne, osa, found, in one of the houses that had been inhabited by the Simba, twelve pages of notes from Brother Lambert Schoenmakers, osc. There he recounts that on May 5, Colonel Makondo had sent him, along with Father Godefrooy, to Baye to print some cards for the colonel with the mission press. But at Baye, the motor for the press gave out, and they were not able to do the work asked for. They returned rapidly to Bondo and there waited for an opportunity to return to Buta.

A few weeks later, someone found yet another series of notes from Brother Lambert that began on August 6, 1964. That which follows completes the journal of Father Jan Verhoeven.

Monday, May 24, 1965

We're back at Buta; on the morning of May 19, a vehicle came to get us at the mission of Bondo. We were able to gather together some things. Brother Leo Ignoul also had to return to Buta. We traveled until we came to the station where some Simba were taken aboard, and that took plenty of time.

After two hours, everything was ready and we could depart in a column: three trucks followed by the major's car. It happened then that we were held back at the last minute for a little while.

We were happy for having crossed the Uele and to be on a truck. But there was no end to the road. The trucks kept on stopping for something; they had to buy some chickens, and then again some marijuana, and then, a little further on, they had to take on some women. We arrived at Likati finally at five o'clock; it took us eight hours to go a little more than thirty-seven miles. We were thinking that since the night was coming on that the Simba would continue their route, but it was nothing like that. They decided to pass the night on the road. They drove us to the mission where there was yet a diocesan priest and a Congolese brother. We felt at home. They would pick us up the following morning, and we would continue to Buta. The next day we had just set out when the vehicle stopped dead, although the driver and the other occupants didn't seem to care. Brother Lambert worked on it a bit, but there was nothing he could do. The other vehicles continued on their course, and the major was going to send another vehicle from Buta immediately to come and get us. And so, back to the mission where we had spent the night.

The next day (May 21), nothing happened. The following day, again nothing was going on, but in the evening, a pickup truck arrived from Bondo, carrying Father Vissers and four sisters who had been to Bangassou; they were not able to cross over the border and so had to turn back. And so in this way, we went back to Buta with them. The driver had been drinking a little and so was tired, and he asked Brother Leo if he wanted to drive; we were very happy about this; we had abandoned our baggage.

It was just getting dark when we left Likati. We had an excellent traveling companion: a native doctor. He kept the Simba interested as he talked about medicine and a certain ceremonial; if a bullet would get them, it would not wound them, but it would transform itself into water. Thanks to this special person, we did not encounter any difficulties at the roadblocks here and there along the route; everywhere we were able to pass immediately even without showing our papers. It was a beautiful night; the trip went smoothly without any problems.

We arrived at Buta on Saturday at midnight, happy to be there again, for we had come to understand that, for the moment, this was the best place for us.

We explained to the colonel the state of the press. I don't think that we should return there.

Tuesday, May 25

During the night, the Simba came to wake up the sisters. They needed (or at least pretended they needed) some sheets and blankets for two ambassadors had arrived, two whites.

Around noon: Some cars arrived at the mission: the colonel, some hereditary chiefs, and also the two whites. We all had to gather round them. The two whites presented themselves as some Egyptian newspaper men. They said that at Leopoldville, they were making the boast that the rebels had assassinated all the whites and all the missionaries, and that now, they saw that we were still living. They were friendly.

We had to stay with them; they took a picture. They then asked the bishop to identify himself and the same for some of us. I think that we would serve for some publicity for the rebels, especially in other countries. A little after their departure, the rifles and machine guns went into action for at least an hour.

Wednesday, May 26

Yesterday evening, when it was already dark out, the same guys who were at our place showed up at the sisters' house. They recounted the same gossip as they had to us. They asked that they be prayed for, for they also desired peace (so they said), and they thought that God would assist them, for they were fighting for a good reason. Of course, they didn't speak of the thousands of innocent victims for whose death they were responsible.

At the sisters' also they made so as to take a picture, and then the comedy ended. Afterward the Simba came here to get some bread and flour, for they had to give their "white visitors" a worthy welcome.

Thursday, May 27

At eight o'clock, there was a Solemn High Mass with three priests. After Mass, a Simba came to see the bishop and gave him a stole that he had stolen someplace.

We learned yesterday evening that General Olenga had tried to kill the president; he unfortunately hit only his arm.

According to what is being bandied about, the National Congolese Army is marching forward; first to see, then to believe.

Friday, May 28

We begin today, the sisters and ourselves, a novena of Masses and rosaries in honor of the Holy Spirit, in order that we may have the courage and the grace to accept everything that we are to undergo.

PART FOUR

Conclusion

Sister M. Eveline had taken some notes in an agenda book. When she was taken to prison the last time, these notes were lost, and when, after one month, she came out of the forest and came back to Buta, she could not find these notes.

So as to complete the diary of Father Jan Verhoeven, osc, she wrote up the following events:

Tuesday, May 18, 1965

It is a question of a second trip to Bangassou in order to seek some provisions and medicines. The colonel also commanded complete sets of equipment for football, and since Father Frans Waldram says that these cannot be found in Bangassou, they receive immediately a furlough of two weeks in order to seek everything at Bangui. The fathers are very happy for this prolonged furlough and will make use of it to get together some provisions in the capital.

Wednesday, May 19

And so today, Fathers Willem Vissers and Frans Waldram departed in the direction of the northern frontier; two white sisters and two black sisters accompanied them. If they departed so quickly, it's surely due to all this famous equipment for football, because usually when the rebels promise a trip for tomorrow, the departure habitually is one month later.

This trip doesn't give us any sense of security, so those of us who remain pray that the travelers arrive safe and sound again at Buta or…to their destination on the other side of the border.

Thursday, May 20

The colonel brings a beautiful package of mail to the mission: news from our families and confreres. A very pleasant surprise.

He is more talkative than ever and says among other things: "If the National Congolese Army arrives here, I will say: 'The missionaries are here, I took good care of them and did not send them away.' " Does he fear that which we are hoping for?

Sunday, May 23

Contrary to expectations, the travelers are already back tonight. They had just arrived at Bangassou when that very morning, Friday, May 21, an order arrived from Bangui, according to which every person who would pass over the border would no longer be able to return. After having presented their case before the competent authorities, assisted by the priests from that place, the travelers received authorization to return, for they had not known about the new regulation just put into effect. Father Frans Waldram, while arguing their case at Bangassou, left immediately for the capital, Bangui, to secure provisions. The others, on their way back, picked up Father Godefrooy and Brother Lambert, who had been absent already for three weeks. They had gone to do some printing at Baye, which they were unable to do because of a breakdown of the printing press. Brother Leo came back with them also, after an equally long absence. His confreres believed that he had already returned to Europe, but the soldiers would not let him pass from Bondo, despite the authorization given by the colonel himself. Father Vissers reports that the army is advancing rapidly in the direction of Buta, which could indicate our long-awaited liberation. But the Crosiers who spent almost three weeks at Bondo were very discouraged by everything that they had to live through and submit to up there. It was so bad that their mood has more influence over the mission than the joy of the liberation that is now at the door.

Monday, May 24

Yesterday, two Egyptians arrived. Today they came to pay a visit to the mission and to the sisters. They present themselves as newspaper reporters, but some say that they are military. They are surprised to encounter so many white missionaries. They think that our presence here is in contradiction with some of the communiqués of the foreign press that say the Simba kill the missionaries and even eat them! Before their departure, they take a photo of the group, or at least they went through the motions.

Thursday, May 27

The communiqués on the radio concerning the National Congolese Army inspire us with a hope that our liberation is very close. Could it be true this time? Could it be this month yet?

Friday, May 28

Today begins the novena in preparation for Pentecost. We pray especially for the courage to accept the decisions of God for us.

Saturday, May 29

It's already afternoon, and there is no one who doubts anymore what is going to happen. We know that the army is getting closer, but when exactly? The fear of that which is going to happen comes to us from the Congolese sisters, and from us, it passes over to the mission. We should stay inside as much as possible, not make any noise, and especially not show that we are happy.

A little after six thirty in the evening, the Simba come to get us and take us to the mission. The fathers and brothers are already outside and seated on the ground in rows of three or four. We have to do the same. They take some rosaries and wristwatches from us, while they continue to howl and throw some little temper tantrums, after which we have to put ourselves in new rows, the fathers and the brothers in front and the rest of us in the back. It's already night. After having run for twenty minutes, we arrive at the police station. All of our purses are searched and returned. When we finally enter the building, we don't have so much as a handkerchief. We sort of arrange ourselves around as best as possible, on the floor or on the windowsills, and so we try to rest a little. All of a sudden, a gang of police barges in: it could be that one or another is still hiding a radio. Of course, the inspection produces nothing. They give us some cigarettes. Someone who gets hold of one fraternally shares it with a companion who was not so fortunate. At our request, we receive also a bottle of water, which is passed from mouth to mouth and then is refilled incessantly. We get settled again for the night, and then there's another interruption. Fifty people in one small room are too many! The sisters have to move, but then two hours later, we are brought back again. Bishop Mbali is there also with two native sisters. The bishop courageously defends himself against certain accusations that the Simba bring up to him; but on the other hand, if they judge him guilty, he is ready to die! The Simba don't really want that, and so he and the two native sisters can leave in peace. Before the bishop departs, the two superiors, Fathers Vissers and Filip Waldram, are also brought up to the tribunal. But it seems that they weren't particularly sought after, so they are able to reintegrate themselves in the group. For the third time we try to get some sleep, but hardly succeed. Some speak a little, but if one speaks, it's in hushed tones with one's neighbor. Father Vissers told us that the fathers were giving each other absolution, in secret, and preparing themselves for the worst.

Sunday, May 30

In mid-morning, the sisters are again led into the same room that they occupied for some little time during the night; they will never again see the fathers and brothers. A Simba informs us of the order of execution for the fathers and brothers, transmitted by telephone from Colonel Makondo Augustine who is fleeing. It is most probable that this was at the same time announced to the fathers and brothers. About five o'clock in the afternoon, a Simba comes to tell us that the death sentence will be executed immediately. The noise and the cries around the prison of the condemned confirm what we had just heard. The fathers and the brothers, stripped naked with their hands tied behind their backs, are led outside. The sad procession is escorted by singing Simba. Coming to the Rubi River, they are killed, one after the other, and the bodies are thrown in the water.

Some rebels wished to spare Brother Lawrence Bosman (a Brother of Saint Gabriel), and they separated him from the others. But not everyone was in agreement, and he was slain right where he stood.

The leg of this last victim was cut just below the knee. A Simba brought it to us. There was no blood, so it was probably cut after his death. We had to touch it, one after the other. It is impossible to say what went on within us, but we were sure that we had before us the relic of a martyr. We know now with certitude: they are, for eternity, in the presence of God.

Tuesday, June 1

Some mercenaries of the National Congolese Army take Buta and find the body of Brother Lawrence already decomposing. They cover it with two truckloads of dirt. There is no trace of the other victims.

Sister M. Eveline van Valkenborgh

THE END

EPILOGUE

Return to Bondo

By Father Ernest Martello, OSC

Beginning a few months after the massacre, some missionaries who had been in Europe began returning, along with some new ones who had never been there before. Because of insecurity, they were obliged to work in the capital city of Kinshasa or in the lower Congo; it took about two years, until 1967, before the first three were allowed to return to their own diocese and to the city of Bondo.

They passed through Buta and went to visit the site of the massacre. It was very emotional. Going on then to Bondo was sad at first, but once they were noticed, they were received like heroes, hoisted on the shoulders of the people and carried through the town.

It was very difficult to begin again. Many people had been killed, among them some of their trusted helpers and teachers. The infrastructure had been badly damaged. There was no furniture any longer in their buildings and schools. The first ones who began teaching sat on their suitcases and used another piece of baggage for a desk. All records of any kind had been destroyed. But they did it; they began again.

Slowly, the idea began to take form of taking Congolese men into the Order. At the very beginning of the mission and for many years following, the rule from Rome for the African missions was that if anyone wanted to become a priest in a religious order, he had first to become a diocesan priest, and then after a time, he might ask to join an order or congregation. The obvious reason for this was to promote and to get going an indigenous diocesan priesthood. Around 1960, the Crosiers had been preparing to establish a novitiate in the Congo, but with the coming of independence and its consequent difficulties and then the Simba rebellion, the idea had been abandoned.

Once things got going again in Bondo, the idea of taking in

Congolese, of implanting the Order in the Congo, began to be considered again, but it always seemed that the situation was not mature enough. One aspect of the Simba rebellion had been a certain demoralizing of the local population and the consequent problems, one of which was the lack of observance of celibacy by some of the local diocesan priests.

In 1983, a decision was made to set up a novitiate in another region of the Congo that seemed morally healthier and where religious vocations were abundant. The then Bishop of Butembo-Beni, Monsignor Emmanuel Kataliko, welcomed the Crosiers to North Kivu, the eastern part of the Congo, in 1984. This is a mountainous region close to the great lakes of Africa and to the countries of Uganda and Rwanda. About 500 miles to the southeast of Bondo, it is an entirely different climate and way of life. Making the trip by car in 1983 took about a week. Now it is virtually impossible, due to the continued degradation and abandonment of the roads in northern Congo.

The Beginning in the Diocese of Butembo-Beni, Province of North Kivu, Democratic Republic of the Congo

From the beginning of their arrival in the Diocese of Butembo-Beni, it was clear that the Crosiers wanted to start afresh with a concentration on their religious life as Crosiers. The Crosiers in Bondo, by the necessity of their task, were *missionaries who were Crosiers.* With this new establishment, the Crosiers knew that they had to turn the corner; now they would be *Crosiers who were missionaries.*

This was necessary if they were to eventually take men into the Order, which was the purpose of this new foundation. The bishop, Monsignor Emmanuel Kataliko, was perfectly in accord with their intention. They were to live their religious life, and thus be a witness to the people, and to undertake whatever works were harmonious with their religious life.

The diocese itself, however, was in a situation where the missionaries who were already there, Augustinians of the Assumption

Sacred Heart Church in Musienene is pictured above. Below: A view of the sanctuary inside Sacred Heart Church. (*Photographs by Prior Provincial Tom Enneking, osc.*)

(commonly called Assumptionists), were getting older, and there were parishes that were now without priests, or very nearly so. Thus, the bishop asked whether the Crosiers could also take care of a large parish while at the same time accentuating their religious life.

The Crosiers agreed and so began at the Parish of the Sacred Heart in Musienene. The first group consisted of three priests and a brother. The practical aspects of accentuating their religious life meant that they wore their habits, at least for Morning Prayer, Mass, and Evening Prayer. The complete French breviary was used, and all the hours were prayed in common. There were a few community prayers such as a decade of the Rosary and a prayer to Blessed Theodore, the founder of the Order, after the noon meal. Meals were of course eaten together. Since they were now in the mountains, the nights were cool, and a fire in the fireplace for evening recreation together felt good. To make community life possible, some aspects of the infrastructure needed repairing, such as a water system and some electricity, and eventually even enlarging the residence.

The parish was very large, at that time having more than twenty-five thousand people with eleven sectors, each with a brick church that might hold anywhere from two hundred to one thousand people. Some of the sectors could be reached by jeep, others by motorcycle, and finally some only by mountain paths. Almost every morning, one of the priests would be *en route* to a sector to begin confessions at six or seven o'clock to be followed by Mass and sometimes marriages. Visits to the sick and meetings with the local parish committee would take place in the afternoons. Most baptisms were done at the main church. At the principal church of the parish, there were three Masses on Sunday in the international African language of Swahili. These Masses would often last the better part of two hours with much singing, dancing, and drumming. Lay people were heavily involved in teaching the faith to the young, in works of charity like the Saint Vincent de Paul Society and the Legion of Mary, and in some aspects of administration. There were, for example, committees made up of the people who decide who is ready to have their child baptized or who is ready to receive the Sacrament of Matrimony.

From the beginning, they held sessions for young people to speak to them about their faith and also to arouse an interest in the religious life. The youth were very responsive. Almost immediately, there was a search for a good place to establish a novitiate.

Finally, a place was found at another parish with no resident pastor, that of Mulo. Once one of the largest parishes of the diocese, it was now one of the smallest because several other parishes had been carved out of it. About eighteen miles south of Musienene, it could be reached in about an hour and a half driving on mountain roads.

The Novitiate at Mulo

Situated on a hillside, surrounded by small mountains that create a beautiful small valley about a mile above sea level, Mulo was a mission built in the traditional manner, with the church and large house for missionaries in the center, with the boys' schools (grades one through twelve) on one side and a convent for the sisters (the Company of Mary Notre Dame—ODN) and schools for the girls (grades one through twelve) on the other side. There was also a house for the priest-teachers of the Assumptionist Congregation alongside the boys' schools. Each of the high schools had large boarding sections at their high point back in the '60s, but by the time of the Crosiers' arrival, the Assumptionists had departed, and the boys' boarding school was a shambles; the girls' boarding school, with better care from the sisters, was still thriving. There were many relics of the former days—a farm with its herd of cows, but now poorly cared for; a large abandoned hog barn; an immense butter churner not used for a long time; the empty cement slab on which the huge generator formerly sat that would give electricity to light all the buildings at night.

The sisters also ran a center for helping poorer people, especially children who were malnourished, serving a hot cereal two or three times a week. The small cheese factory was still in operation and made two bricks of cheese a day.

The bishop gave the Crosiers five buildings that formerly had been used by the Assumptionists. A neighboring parish at Lubero was also served by the Crosiers for a few years but later was given back to the diocese.

The first Crosier community in Mulo consisted of three priests:

Above: Now part of the Priory of Chipukizi in Mulo, this is one of the buildings that had been built by the Assumptionists and was given to the Crosiers by the bishop. Below: The parish church in Mulo as viewed from the road.
(Photographs by Prior Provincial Tom Enneking, osc.)

one was the pastor of the parish, one was the director of novices, and the third was the assistant director of novices. The director of novices served as the superior of the group. The first novitiate with five Congolese novices began on September 13, 1986. Though close to the style of life followed at Musienene, there were adaptations for the novitiate. The day would begin at six o'clock in the morning with the recitation of the Angelus, since the church bell had been rung at that time for decades already. This was followed by Morning Prayer, meditation, and then Mass with the parishioners in the parish church. Later, once the Crosiers had built their own priory church, they began to have daily Conventual Eucharist together, going to the parish church only on Sundays.

The schedule established then remains in effect today. Daily Conventual Eucharist is celebrated in French with virtually all of the hymns sung in various African languages. The Office of Readings is celebrated at noon in religious habit followed by a decade of the rosary. The Mid-afternoon Prayer (the old *None* in Latin) is celebrated at three o'clock, preceded by the special Crosier Passion Prayer. The first psalm at this prayer is most often sung in Swahili in African psalm tone. Evening Prayer is often as late as possible, giving the novices enough time to play football on Wednesday and Friday afternoons (with music practices on Wednesdays and Saturdays), since the sun sets between six and seven o'clock. Supper follows. After the novices finish the dishes and peel the potatoes for the next day, there is recreation until eight thirty, followed by Night Prayer.

From the beginning, there were separate recreation rooms for the solemnly professed and the novices, each with their own fire. Mulo is higher in altitude than Musienene and thus colder at night and cooler during the day.

Each day, the novices have a half-hour of *lectio divina* (personal Bible reading with prayer in their rooms), several classes on spirituality and the life of the Order, and several hours of manual labor. From the beginning, there was a great effort to get the novices involved in keeping the gardens necessary for food and the raising of rabbits, chickens, ducks, and turkeys for more protein in the diet. In the early years, this was complemented by courses in cooking, car repair (changing a tire, etc.), and some wood working (to help them learn to build rabbit cages, for example). Now the curriculum has changed a bit, but the old emphasis of getting the novices involved in manual labor continues.

Though a good beginning had been made, one evening after about nine months, the first five novices abruptly departed. This was a big shock. They all came back the next day, but the superior wisely informed them that they had made their decision, and that if they wanted to come back, they would have to reapply and go through the whole discernment process again. No one did. Looking back at it, one could probably say that the novices were looking for educational advantages and more freedom to do what they wanted. The superiors were adept at understanding this and dealt with it firmly. Even though the whole first group had departed, all was not lost. There had been three postulants preparing for the next year's novitiate, and they immediately presented themselves. Thus a new novitiate year began with three novices on September 13, 1987, and at the same time, eight postulants moved into the postulant house. A priest to teach philosophy and a brother to direct the renovation and building programs were added to the community.

The following year, the first year of philosophy began for the novices in their second year, and seven postulants were accepted into the novitiate. The eighth had died of a twisted bowel, virtually on the eve of his investiture. He was buried in the Crosier habit but in his own village cemetery at a place near Mulo called Masereka.

The next year, the three novices who had completed their two years of novitiate made their first profession of vows on September 14, 1988, the Solemnity of the Exaltation of the Cross, the principal feast of the Crosier Fathers and Brothers, whose official name is Canons Regular of the Order of the Holy Cross. The following years were years of slowly building up the group. One year, there were no novices. There were few novices in other years. But eventually, a five-year educational program was established in Mulo for the acceptance and training of Crosier fathers and brothers.

"Chipukizi"

"Chipukizi" (pronounced: cheepookeezee) is a word in Swahili that refers to an old stump of a tree that has now begun to sprout again. After several years of searching for the right word, this word was chosen as the name for the Crosier Community in Mulo. Its symbolism is rich in meaning for the community, because in the acceptance of novices into the Order, the Crosiers consider this growth to be the fruit of the sacrifice of the martyrs. The pictures of the twenty-three who gave their lives at Dakwa and Buta are arranged in the back of the novitiate chapel along with this text in Swahili: "Unless a grain of wheat falls into the ground and dies, it remains just a grain of wheat; but if it dies it produces much fruit (Jn 12:24). The martyrs are the patrons of the house. It is this same symbolism that is contained in the title of this volume: "The blood of the martyrs is the seed of the faith."

The Crosier Fathers and Brothers in the Democratic Republic of the Congo 2012

By God's grace, a lot has been accomplished since 1920 and even since 1984 with the first establishment in the Diocese of Butembo-Beni and the acceptance of the first novice class in 1986. There have been twenty-three men ordained priests, though sadly Father Erasmus Manzekele died after only one year of ordination, and there are five brothers who have completed their training. More than seventy-five more men are in various stages of the eleven years of training to become Crosier fathers and brothers, including eight postulants. This means close to 100 Congolese men wear the Crosier habit.

The Crosier region has been established as a proprovince with the title "The Martyrs of Bondo." It remains under the European Province until it can become a full province within the Order. A Congolese has been elected as prior proprovincial. The first priory at Mulo, with the name "Chipukizi," was established in 2007, and a Congolese was elected the prior. Before it can become a full province, two more houses must reach the status of a priory. Sadly, the Crosiers had to leave the Diocese of Bondo in 1993 due to diminishment of the number of priests and brothers available. All of the Crosier foreign missionaries have left the proprovince and have returned to their home province.

Crosier Apostolic Presence in the Democratic Republic of the Congo

Bondo, Province of Orientale

What can be said of Bondo now that the Crosiers have left? It continues under the leadership of an African bishop, some diocesan priests, and some members of missionary religious communities. The Crosiers spent seventy-three years there. How much they labored, traveling through the bush, staying in the most primitive places without the comforts of home! Seventy-three years of prayer and of celebrating the sacraments; of teaching catechumens; of working with youth in the schools and workshop; of hard manual labor, constructing churches, schools, and residences for missionaries; in effect, seventy-three years of bringing Jesus and His new life to the people there. They gave their very lives. More than one hundred Crosiers served in the Diocese of Bondo over the period of seventy-three years. There are fourteen graves in Bondo of Crosiers who died there, many of them in the early years when they had no remedies for tropical diseases. You can see their ages in the elenchus of deceased confreres: they died at the ages of 32, 35, 37, 46, 47, 48, etc. Only God knows the effect of their work and sacrifice, as the seed of His new life was planted in the hearts of so many people. The value of their planting endures in the hearts of the new generation also. The Crosiers of Bondo are not just a memory; they live in the hearts of all those who live the life of Jesus now.

Likewise, the legacy of the twenty-three martyrs continues to bear fruit there and elsewhere.

Musienene, North Kivu

The Crosiers continue to serve this large parish, which has tripled in population since the Crosiers first took charge of it, but now several sectors have been created into autonomous parishes with other religious groups in charge of them. Besides the parish, there are several schools and houses of religious communities of sisters and brothers that the Crosiers serve. The Crosiers have initiated

Above: A hydroelectric plant in Musienene uses water from a small river to create electricity. At right: Machinery inside the hydroelectric plant generates electricty for the center and surrounding area. (Photographs by Prior Provincial Tom Enneking, osc.)

an alphabetization program for adults; a library for the parish; and a women's support group for those abused, especially by the military. They have constructed a large multipurpose hall and several classrooms for religious programs, and recently initiated a project to help those poor who seem to be the most down-and-out. They also provide twenty-four-hour ambulance service. In all of these projects, they have been assisted by benefactors in Europe and the United States.

Down the road about a mile from the parish, the Crosiers purchased a twenty-four-acre tract of land, part of an old tea plantation, and have gradually been improving it. This terrain was called in the local language "Mutinga." Out of old colonial ruins, a beautiful new house has been built for five Crosiers, and it is here that the proprovincial resides. The main enterprise-apostolate is a Center for Rural Development called CEPRORUMA (*Centre Promotion Rurale—Matumaini)*, the aim of which is to improve the life of the people. "Matumaini" is Swahili for a "hope that is already plugged

Above: The formation house for men in vows studying at Holy Cross College is built on terraces. Left: The priory chapel is used by the novices and the community. Below left: Wood is chopped and stacked. A generator provides electricity only from 6-10 p.m., so the cooking is done on wood fires.

(Photographs by Prior Provincial Tom Enneking, osc.)

into the future." This center includes a tree nursery and experimental projects for the development of better vegetables and new breeds of rabbits, chickens, pigs, and cows. There is a carpentry shop, a tailor shop, and room for other sorts of projects. One cannot miss the flour mill where women are frequently lined up with their sacks of grain to be ground into flour. The latest improvement has been a hydroelectric plant in a small river that provides the electricity necessary for the house and the various projects. Still to be added is a conference center devoted to rural development.

Mulo, North Kivu

Priory and Parish

At this site is found the Parish of Saint Theresa the Little Flower, the Priory of Chipukizi, the postulancy program for those asking admittance to the Order, and the novitiate (the spiritual year for introduction into the life of the Order). The priory building is very large with three large courtyards and an impressive chapel that seats two hundred people. Across the road and a mile down a beautiful drive shaded by trees is another residence for those seminarians who have made their first profession of vows in the Order. The site is named for the hill that it is on, "Katwa-Kabakwe." It is also considered part of the Priory of Chipukizi and has its own chapel dedicated to Saint Odilia, Patroness of the Order, which seats about one hundred fifty people. Life here is much the same as in the novitiate except that there is more time allotted to classes and study.

Farm

The farm here is large enough for about forty head of cattle and has stables for pigs, chickens, sheep, rabbits, ducks, and turkey. Quinine trees are cultivated for the bark, which is sold for the making of medicines in Europe. There is a tree nursery and a program to replace the trees cut for firewood. Other enterprises include a large carpentry shop; a place for the fabrication of bricks and roof tile (clay); and a small dairy that produces milk, yogurt, and cheese.

Besides the farm at the priory, the Crosiers have also purchased a tract of land at Kighali further into the interior (going west toward the great rainforest), which can now be reached entirely by car or truck, since the Crosiers themselves have completed a new road. Though abandoned there for a while due to attacks by rebel groups, the school and dispensary are functioning again because of the Crosiers' help. They hope eventually to move some cattle and goats down there and to continue a quinine tree plantation.

Holy Cross College

The seminary program, which follows the spiritual year of novitiate, consists of three years of philosophy and other studies that make for a well-rounded liberal arts college program. At insistent demands from a few individuals, the doors were opened in 1998 to admit laymen who were seeking a college education and who were willing to follow the seminary curriculum. The first such student was a married man with eight children. Others followed. The school had already been affiliated with the Assumptionist Seminary in Butembo so that the students could receive a college diploma. Later, on its own merits, it was accredited by the Major Superiors of Men's Religious Orders. Finally, it was accredited by the Congolese State in 2006 with the right to grant its own diplomas. The Congolese State, however, insisted on adding other faculties besides philosophy. It was immediately decided to add, as soon as possible, a clinical psychology program, followed by physical technology and agriculture-veterinary faculties.

A campus separated from the priory and seminary living quarters had already been begun. Now, besides a classroom building, there is a large library complex and an administration building, with an auditorium under construction.

The clinical psychology faculty is unique on this side of the country. The great need for such a program was seen because of the masses of people traumatized by the recurring wars that began in 1996. The root cause of these conflicts seems to be the minerals, such as coltan used in the making of cell phones and computers, diamonds, and gold. As long as the wars go on, the minerals pass over the borders and onto the world markets much more easily. Because of the political situation that is too complex to explain here, various militias prey on the people because often they are unpaid and have no

Above: Students at Holy Cross College in Mulo take notes during class. At right: Many of the books in the college's library were obtained from Europe through the efforts of Ernest Martello, osc. (*Photographs by Prior Provincial Tom Enneking, osc.*)

Above: The interior of the Parish of St. Theresa the Little Flower in Mulo.
Below: The auditorium at Holy Cross College in Mulo remains to be finished.
(Photographs by Prior Provincial Tom Enneking, osc.)

provisions of their own. Besides the frequent looting, the sexual abuse of women has become a systematic way of eroding family life and destroying the will of the people. Women of all ages are abused, and they are often shunned by their families due to traditional mores and the fear of disease. The gravity of the situation was noted in the fall 2009 report of a meeting of the Presbyteral Council of the Diocese of Butembo-Beni:

> The lack of security in which we find ourselves is alarming: we continue to count the number of homes burned down, right now about 1500, of women who have been raped, of men taken by force to carry booty or taken as hostages, of children struck down in the bush, of people killed, of bodies not buried which lie rotting and risk causing an outbreak of cholera, of thousands of people displaced among whom are women and children as well as elderly. And this all has consequences: schools are abandoned and of course the students don't get an education, sanitary structures are completely destroyed...All of these flagrant violations of human rights and the destruction of nature, are these not all crimes? What kind of society are we passing on to our children?

It is the goal of the clinical psychology faculty to respond to the need for emotional healing of so many people harmed by their experiences in this situation. In effect, Holy Cross College wishes to develop therapists and professionals capable of accompanying and of assisting persons who live through these traumatizing events. It also wishes to form professionals capable of alleviating the insufficiencies in the school milieu.

Along with Holy Cross College and its clinical psychology faculty, the Crosiers have begun the Center for Listening and Accompaniment to assist people who need to talk about their experiences and to receive help. (Since the word "counseling" does not exist in French, the word "listening" is used.) The Listening and Accompanying Center is more and more frequented, and a separate residence has now been found for it. The same therapists who teach in the college also work in the center. The professors at the college also organize the psychology students for group work in the villages to help change mentalities and to identify people who need psychological help as well as to develop teams in the village that can respond to the various needs for healing.

The plan is to begin master's degree programs in clinical and school psychology as well as in philosophy in the near future. There are a total of forty-six part-time and full-time faculty members lecturing at Holy Cross College. The student population is around sixty. In the first year, of the twenty registered for psychology, eight were women. The functioning of the college up to now has been due to donations from the United States and Europe as well as the payment of tuition by the students. Currently the tuition is $300 per year. A student can live comfortably for about $1300, including room, board and other expenses. Evidently, the student enrollment must grow if the college is going to continue and to develop the other faculties of physical technology and agriculture-veterinary.

Butembo, North Kivu

Butembo is a dusty city with more than two hundred thousand inhabitants and a thriving commercial center. All the coltan (two minerals used in making cell phones), diamonds, gold, and who knows what else, pass through Butembo. It cannot be found on the old maps, because it used to be smaller than the nearby colonial cities of Beni and Lubero, but it has grown in the past thirty years or so. One can find a million-dollar home (or at least what looks like it to us) next to many simple homes of the townspeople made of branches, mud, and thatch. There are splendid looking banks going up, but there is not a paved street in the city, no central water system or sewage system, and no central electricity. It is all still in the making. You can buy just about anything you want here as the merchants are often off to Dubai or other cities in Asia on shopping trips. It has been said that next to the capital city of Kinshasa, Butembo is the next in line of importance, far surpassing the old colonial cities of Kisangani (the old Stanleyville) or Lubumbashi (the old Elizabethville).

About ten years ago the Crosiers purchased a large hill (about twelve acres) on the east side of the city of Butembo with the intention of establishing a house there that might serve as a residence for the provincial superior, students attending the university, and later a retreat center along with a church. A house is now built, but the need has arisen to send Crosier seminarians to another seminary besides the one in Kinshasa, and so the house in Butembo has begun as a residence for those seminarians studying theology at Saint Octave, the diocesan major seminary of Butembo. Through the help of an American benefactor, the Crosiers have established a system for water that helps the surrounding neighborhoods. A large spring has been tapped in the surrounding mountains and is piped down to the Crosier hill, which has been named Saint Helena, from where it goes out to the neighborhoods and can be obtained by the people at centralized faucets. This hill and house hold much promise for the future apostolic presence of the Crosiers to people of the city of Butembo.

Kinshasa, Capital City of the Democratic Republic of the Congo

Kinshasa is the capital city of the Democratic Republic of the Congo. This is the old Leopoldville from colonial days, and there are still many high-walled/fenced-in villas as well as miles and miles of poor neighborhoods in this sprawling city of perhaps ten million people. The city is built right alongside the great Congo River, which at this point is extremely wide and bears the name Stanley Pool after the explorer Stanley. From here, the river flowing west begins its forty-mile trajectory of cascading falls down to the city of Matadi, where it is again navigable out to the Atlantic Ocean. The capital for the other Congo Republic (a former French colony and much smaller country), which bears the name Brazzaville, is right across the river from Kinshasa. Due to the immense expanse between the two cities, there is as yet no bridge connecting the two cities, though there is some boat traffic.

Automobile traffic is heavy on the main streets of Kinshasa, which are paved. There are not many traffic lights in evidence, but there are policemen at major intersections. It is impossible to describe the immense activity and excitement and all the people in the streets and on the sidewalks of the city of Kinshasa. You can see bread for sale everywhere; buy cooked omelets, roasted meat, fruit, ice cream, and drinks of all sorts; and see thousands of items for sale everywhere. On a corner, you might even spot a kid taking a bath out of a bucket.

Besides being home to the president of the country and the central government of the Democratic Republic of the Congo, this is also the residence of Laurent Cardinal Monsengwo Pasinya. Kinshasa unifies the Congo not only politically but also ecclesially, since there are many church offices here that serve the entire Catholic Church in the Congo. The papal nuncio has his residence here, and there is a large inter-diocesan center with services for all the dioceses, of which there are almost fifty, several of them being archdioceses. The Catholic Church had founded the University of the Congo, but since its nationalization by the dictator Mobutu in the 1970s, the church has found it necessary to establish its own Catholic faculties for higher studies in philosophy, theology, and the social sciences. Bishops send their priests, seminarians, and lay people here from all over the country.

The Crosiers came in 1991 and established a residence for their seminarians who could then study at the Oblate of Mary School of Theology, which in effect serves several religious communities. Normally, the Crosier seminarian will spend four years here, before beginning his two in-service years prior to his priestly ordination. During the summers, the seminarians receive assignments to parishes where they live for a few weeks to put to use some of the theology that they've been studying.

The community residence of the Crosiers consists of four dwellings on about a half-acre of land surrounded by a high wall in the middle of the city. Two of the dwellings had been middle class family homes, and two dormitory-type structures were constructed by the Crosiers. The large living room of one of the houses serves as the chapel, and other larger rooms in the two homes serve as a dining room and recreation room. Because the city cannot maintain adequately all its utilities, there is not sufficient water and electricity.

"Street kids" are to be found all over in Kinshasa. They have no home except the streets. Some of them may be orphans, while others are suspected of being possessed by the devil and so are thrown out of their homes by their parents. Quasi-Christian sects that emphasize possession by and exorcism of the devil abound in Kinshasa. With funds from benefactors in Europe, the first Crosier superior here established a small home for "street kids." The Crosiers eventually purchased a property about a half-block from their own residence where they built a nice home that can house about fifteen. The name of the house is "Mboka Bolingani," which means "Center of Brotherly Love." The Crosiers employ a full-time director, a cook, and a night watchman, while one of the Crosiers is placed in direct charge of the home. The children may range in age from seven to eighteen. During the day they go out to school. One goal of this apostolate is to have the children return to their families when possible.

THE BEGINNING

Thus it is that what seemed to be the end of something in the massacre of twenty-three Crosiers in 1965 we see was really a new beginning of the Order in Africa. "The blood of the martyrs is indeed the seed of the faith." A song composed by the first Congolese Crosiers says: "Those martyrs followed Christ. The seed buried in the earth, yes truly bears much fruit. Our Order preaches the Cross. The martyrs' witness teaches us to be faithful until death."

APPENDIX

AN INTERVIEW WITH BROTHER MARCEL SMITS, OSC

Conducted by Father Ernest Martello, OSC

This interview was conducted in 1990 for the 25th anniversary of the massacre. It is repeated here for the useful information it gives in relation to the diary of Crosier Father Jan Verhoeven, osc.

Brother Marcel, you were in the Congo during the period of the Simba Rebellion, 1964–1965. Was the Simba a communist movement?

Absolutely. Chinese communist inspired. I was often called on to repair jeeps and trucks and other equipment for them, and I would see from time to time the Chinese markings on the supplies they were receiving.

What were the Simba like?

Their system was to recruit soldiers from all over and then to send them to serve or fight in another part of the country. Thus the Simba in our area had no family or tribal connections with the local population. The same of course goes for the commanding officers. Because they had no special feelings for the local people, they could be tough and ruthless. They conscripted youth and made all kinds of promises to them. A few were volunteers, but the majority of them were forced into service.

They employed witch doctors in their training. These witch doctors made use of fetishes to protect the soldiers, and they convinced them that the enemies' bullets could not harm them. The officers used blanks in their rifles to demonstrate that they could not be harmed by bullets. They also used drugs to make themselves feel invulnerable.

In their first skirmishes with the National Congolese Army, they were very successful. Because of the drugs and their beliefs in their invulnerability, they were extremely aggressive, even chanting as they charged the enemy. When one of them was hit by enemy bullets, he could keep on advancing. He was on drugs, and so he felt no pain. This phenomenon gave rise to the belief among the soldiers of the National Congolese Army that the Simba were indeed invulnerable! They were completely routed by the Simba advances. It was for this reason that the president of the Congo, Mr. Tschombe, called on the South African and Belgian mercenaries to lead the fight against the Simba. United Nations troops had been in the country earlier to help restore order in other parts, but they had already left, thinking their job was done. The Simba rebellion was just beginning.

What was it like when the Simba first came to Bondo?

We, the missionaries, had no idea of their coming. But evidently they already had sympathizers in the local population because the day they arrived there was an arc of flowers put up in the main street for them. The first group was comprised of only six or seven soldiers who were welcomed as "liberators." At first, we thought it was the National Congolese Army. We had never heard of the Simba. We had heard of some military and political difficulties at Buta but figured it was the national army causing trouble with the population.

There were several executions at Bondo, and you were forced to be present at some of these, correct?

Yes. Immediately after independence in 1960 there were many political parties and attempts to do all sorts of things. One party, that of Patrice Lumumba, had communist sympathies. When the Simba arrived in Bondo, they already had lists of the members of the other parties. Teachers, businessmen, and local politicians who had worked hard to move the country in other directions were executed. The missionaries were forced to be present at some of these.

What was the mood of the missionaries during the first days of the Rebellion?

When it first began, we thought it was a revolution confined to the army alone. Later, we thought it was a political movement to rid the government of corruption. Finally, with the first executions, we saw that the leaders were criminally minded. They killed perfectly innocent people for no other reason than that they belonged to another political party. We observed that the soldiers were often high on drugs. It quickly became a very tense situation. We didn't know what to expect. At any moment, we were gathered together and forced to attend an execution or to repair this or that for them. Sometimes they would come and begin searching the house. Once they found an old Belgian flag that was in some barrels along with old clothes that we saved to give away to people. They began to rant and rave, and for a while, we thought that they might shoot us on the spot. One of them began to insist that we eat it. The commander finally said that if we walked on it, that would be sufficient.

Was there a unity among the missionaries at this time, or did you dispute about things? Were there some who were pillars of strength for the others?

There was a strong unity among us from the very beginning to help each other survive and to do the best we could to help the local people survive. There were no pillars of strength as such. We all changed from day to day. Someone who was timid on one occasion was brave the next, and vice versa.

Did you ever meet Gbenye, the president of the Simba rebel republic?

Yes. The South African mercenaries' first entry into our area came in September 1964, though they did not reach Bondo. Some of them were captured by the Simba. When Stanleyville was retaken by the Simba, Gbenye ordered that the mercenaries be brought to Stanleyville. Our commander misinterpreted the word "mercenary" for "missionary," and hence transported us by truck to Stanleyville, a trip of several days.

Along the way, close to Stanleyville, we had stopped for a rest, and then another car came by and stopped. It was Gbenye himself. The soldiers were surprised and jumped to attention. He asked what we were doing there; we then found out it was a mistake. Later, we were taken to his house, and he told us to return to Bondo and to continue life as normal. He wanted the schools and the parishes to function. After we told him that much of our equipment and supplies had been stolen or ruined by his soldiers, he ordered money for each mission station.

So all the Simba weren't necessarily against the missionaries?

Oh no. We had three or four different commanders at Bondo. Some were cruel, but not all. The last, Colonel Augustine Makondo, who is the one accused of giving the order for the execution of the missionaries, was generally benevolent. I don't think that he ordered the execution; rather, I think it came from higher up. He had been educated at the military school in Liege, Belgium, and knew our Order at Hannut. He never was directly against us. He promised us several times that he would not harm us.

I was a mechanic, and he needed me to keep his jeeps and trucks going. I knew him well and tried to use my influence to help protect as many as possible in the local situation. That's how it came about that I left on vacation. He was so proud of the fact that he had jeeps and trucks running, when the other commanders had much more difficulty in keeping their equipment going. Of course, I also sometimes sabotaged vehicles—in such a way that they wouldn't realize that it was I who did it.

One day, after I had fixed a jeep, I was driving it around, as I often did, to use these opportunities to go around town and to check on people, the sisters for example, and to search for supplies. He stopped me so that he could show off the jeep to someone. He told me then: "I'm sending you on vacation." He repeated it several times, but I never believed it.

One day, however, a car and chauffeur arrived with orders that

I was wanted by the commander. I went. Sister Paula was there, too. He was sending us both on vacation to Belgium by way of Bangassou in the Central African Republic, the country directly above us and whose borders we were close to. We asked if we could take another sister along who was ill. He gave permission, and we left immediately. We asked how we could bypass the Simba en route. He said that the chauffeur was his right-hand man and that we would have no difficulty. All went well. At Bangassou, the superior of the Holy Spirit Fathers, whom we knew well, speeded us on our way to Brussels.

While I was in Europe, I visited all the families of those missionaries in prison. At that time we thought that everyone would still be liberated.

If not all the Simba were against the missionaries and Makondo was even benevolent at times, why did they use you as hostages?

As soon as the Simba learned that their former "invincible" power was breaking down as a result of the action of the white mercenaries from Belgium and South Africa, they figured that if they took us as hostages, that this would stop the mercenaries' advance. That's why we were imprisoned at various times and hauled around from place to place. It depended on where the mercenaries were; they tried to use us as a buffer.

How did it come about that you went back to the Congo?

As I was leaving the Congo with the two sisters, the chauffeur—a trustee of Makondo—told us not to think about coming back, that it would all be over in a few weeks. While in Europe, I did not say this to anyone. I tried to keep alive the hopes of the families for an eventual release.

After a couple of months, our bishop, Monsignor Creemers, osc, received a message from the superior of the Holy Spirit Fathers at Bangassou that said he had information that things were very tense at Buta, and that perhaps if I returned I could help calm down the commander and save the situation.

In my own mind, I did not believe that I could help. I figured that when I returned, if they were going to kill us, they would kill us all. But of course, I didn't know. So I decided without hesitation that, of course, I would go back. The bishop came and helped explain things to my family. We were all agreed that I should try it. I left immediately. Sister Paula insisted on going back with me.

When we arrived at Bangassou, it was impossible to cross the border to re-enter the Congo, because the Simba on the Congo side of the river had fired across and killed some people on the Central African Republic side. Thus everything was sealed off. We went immediately to Bangui, the capital of the Central African Republic, because we knew there was a pilot there who did some surveillance for the mercenaries. While there, we met Father Frans Waldram, osc, who had been let out to get provisions for the others. He was in the same situation that we were, unable to return. The pilot told us that the mercenaries were ready to march on Buta and Bondo and that we should not try to go back. Father Waldram and I were not satisfied and decided that we would try to cross the river in a canoe, despite the fact that the pilot told us that we would probably be stopped on the Central African Republic side. We were determined to go ahead. He then told us to listen to the radio, and if we heard the words "the suitcase is open," that would mean the march on Buta had begun. If we heard the "suitcase is closed," that would mean that it had been delayed. We left to cross the river—a distance of about one hundred fifty miles to the border. We stopped at a mission post we knew to eat, and while there we listened to the radio. It was then that we heard the words "the suitcase is open." Just a little later it was announced that the fathers and brothers at Buta had been killed. The pilot had seen their white cassocks lying on the river bank. Of course we were crushed and broke down immediately.

We went back to Bangassou where we received confirmation of the massacre, and also the information that the sisters had been taken into the bush by the Simba in flight but then abandoned. They were unharmed. We wanted to go back there to help them, but we were told that they were taken care of, and that it was impossible to return to Bondo and Buta at this time. So, we left for Brussels on June 4.

Of course, the arrival at the airport in Brussels was extremely emotional. There were hundreds of people there, many reporters among them. The chaplain of the airport quickly ushered us into his office and helped us to select questions to answer.

You were among the first of the Crosiers to return to Bondo several months later. What was that like?

There were three of us in the first group to return. In fact, we waited a long time—for months—in Kinshasa, because there were still Simba in the area. In the meantime we received all kinds of provisions from Europe; people were extremely generous in giving us all kinds of supplies to get started.

Finally, we went first to Buta to see where the others had been killed. Of course, it was extremely emotional.

Going to Bondo was sad at first, but it soon became a very happy occasion. We were received like emperors—hoisted on the shoulders of the people and carried through the city. Many of our friends were still there.

I think that the people felt a little guilty, that perhaps they hadn't done enough to protect us. That's not true, but perhaps they felt that way, and so they didn't expect us back. And so when we did arrive, it was a real homecoming. My idea from the first was that we should forget the past and get started again. That's what we did.

Acknowledgments

The Crosier Fathers and Brothers gratefully acknowledge the contributions of Susan Wolff for her editorial assistance in the first English draft of this work and of Carrie Powell for editing and designing the final product. Father James Remmerswaal, osc, provided valuable translation assistance by enabling the translator and editor to check their work against the original Dutch edition. We also thank the Crosier Province of Blessed Theodore de Celles for allowing us to use photographs of the martyrs and other snapshots from this time period.

The cover was designed by Br. José Velázquez Filiberto, osc, a novice of the Provice of St. Odilia. Father Gene Plaisted, osc, and Gary Feldhege provided assistance to Br. José. The Crosiers are very grateful for their creative work.